FLY-FISHING
with
CHILDREN

❧

A GUIDE FOR PARENTS

FLY-FISHING
with
CHILDREN

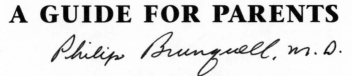

A GUIDE FOR PARENTS

Philip Brunquell, m.d.

Philip Brunquell, M.D.

Foreword by
Tom Rosenbauer

The Countryman Press
Woodstock · Vermont

THE COUNTRYMAN PRESS, INC.
P.O. Box 175 · Woodstock, Vermont 05091

Copyright © 1994 by Philip Brunquell
Foreword copyright © 1994 by Tom Rosenbauer

Library of Congress Cataloging-in-Publication Data

Brunquell, Philip.
Fly-fishing with children : a guide for parents / Philip Brunquell ; foreword by Tom Rosenbauer.
     p.   cm.
ISBN 0-88150-289-8
1. Fly fishing. 2. Fly fishing—Study and teaching. I. Title.
SH456.B725   1994
799.1'1—dc20   93–51027   CIP

Printed in the United States of America
10 9 8 7 6 5 4 3 2

Cover photograph by Brooks Dodge © 1992
Cover design by Karen Savary / Text design by Sally Sherman
Line art in figures 2.4, 3.4, 4.1, 4.4, 5.3, 8.3, 8.6, 10.1, 10.2, and 10.3 by
Karen Savary; line art in appendices A and C © 1994 by
Patti Zimmerman, Wisteria Graphics

Knot diagrams and tying instructions in figures 3.1, 3.2, and 3.3 provided by Stren Fishing Lines, 6327 Brandywine Bldg., Wilmington, DE 19898. Knot and loop drawings in figures 3.5 and 3.6 are reproduced, with permission, from the *Book of Knots*, published by Ande Monofilament, 1310 53rd Street, West Palm Beach, FL 33407. The photographs in figures 3.9 and 3.10 and the information on which the illustration in figure 4.4 is based were kindly provided by E. J. "Dutch" Schaefers of Terminal Tactics, Inc. Illustrations and instructions for the sliding bobber technique in figure 4.3, originally published in *Fly Fisherman* magazine, are reproduced by kind permission of Dave Whitlock. Hook removal illustrations and instructions in figure 5.5 were provided by O. Mustad and Son (USA), Inc., P.O. Box 838, 247–253 Grant Avenue, Auburn, NY 13021. pH scale illustration in figure 10.1 is based on information provided by the Fish and Wildlife Service of the US Department of the Interior. All other credits are shown with the appropriate illustrations. Photographs not otherwise credited are by the author.

The essay "Ties of Affection" in Chapter 8 is reprinted by kind permission of Craig Nova and the New York Times Company. Material in Chapter 4 on troll-walking, paraphrased from S. R. Slaymaker's book *Simplified Fly Fishing*, is included with permission from Stackpole Books, 5067 Ritter Road, Mechanicsburg, PA 17055 (1-800-732-3669), which publishes a paperback edition.

for Amy and Christopher,
my love,
my life

*"...the patience of the adult must exceed
the attention span of the child."*

—William G. Tapply
*Those Hours Spent Outdoors:
Reflections on Hunting and Fishing,*
Charles Scribner's Sons
New York, 1988

ↄ

CONTENTS

APPENDICES

FOREWORD

Rarely have I met someone I more admire than Phil Brunquell. We first met over the telephone, the morning after he received a copy of the *Orvis News* which asked for help in distributing fly-tying kits to hospitalized children. I think the ink was still wet on Phil's copy as he dialed, and in a matter of days this energetic doctor had organized a fly-tying weekend around these kits for kids with lower body paralysis. Next he gained the enthusiastic support of fellow members of the Connecticut Fly Fishermen's Association, to come to the Newington Children's Hospital and work with the kids in the psychiatric ward. It soon became a labor of love for the volunteers as well as the children, and Phil was the driving force who kept the volunteers interested and the hospital administration supportive. This was an after-hours volunteer project for a doctor who works with kids with illnesses of all types day in and day out, with two young children of his own at home. If Phil heard you say that, his response would likely be that unlike him, the kids don't get to go home and get away from it.

If this book only took advantage of Phil's professional and personal insights about teaching children, it would be a worthwhile addition to your home reference library. Instead, it is a gem that will far exceed your expectations. Its precise language and vibrant voice will make you want to jump out of your chair, hug your kids, and take them fly-fishing. If you think that by reading this book you are only going to learn how to teach your kids to fish with a fly, you'll be pleasantly surprised to find many perceptive and innovative ways to look at tackle selection, casting, knots, and presentation—for fly-fishers of any age and any level of experience. But whatever you learn for yourself will be just a windfall. Phil never loses sight of his goal in this book: To bring parent and child closer together in a patient, loving way; to help them share an outdoor experience and to develop an environmental ethic together.

If I could add anything to this fine book I guess it would be a caution about pacing. I have seen too many children turn their backs on fly-fishing because one or both parents wanted to share it with their child so much that they pushed too hard, and the kids, as they will, pushed back. I almost made the mistake of going to the other extreme with my own daughter, Brooke. I never encouraged her about any aspect of fishing; in fact I waited for her to beg to be in my lap to tie flies when she was four. Now we go fishing only when she asks me, even though we have a trout stream across from the house and a productive bluegill pond ten minutes away.

When we fish, we take either the fly-rod or a Mickey Mouse spin-cast rod: Her call. I cast, she reels in the fish, and this routine was all right with her until a bluegill fishing trip this summer. Sitting in the bow of a canoe like an oversized dragonfly, outfitted with adult-sized polarized glasses and baseball hat, she could actually watch bluegills take poppers for the first time. Inspired, she asked to try this casting stuff (I had never even asked her if she wanted a casting lesson, planning to try to interest her when she was eight or nine.) I handed her the rod, ducked, and hoped her long hair would at least keep the fly clear of the back of her head. Luckily, Brooke inherited her mother's hand-eye coordination, not her father's, and I hoped she had been watching me carefully.

The rod tip moved to twelve o'clock, past one o'clock, and continued to almost dinnertime before it suddenly thrashed forward, clearing Brooke, me, and the canoe in one miraculous wide loop. It fell to the water with the bluegill bug resting in the center of a coil of line, rocking seductively in the waves created by all that fly line landing in one spot. A bluegill nosed up to the fly and kissed it, holding onto the fly in an unbluegill-like fashion, just long enough for Brooke to set the hook somehow. (I don't remember how she did it; since I had never prepared for this moment I was still in a state of shock that she had hooked a fish on her very first unassisted cast.) She reeled the fish in and I unhooked it trying not to make too big a deal of the past few seconds, a sure way to kill six-year-old enthusiasm.

The next time we go fishing, I may try a little more formal instruction, fully two years before I had intended to start it. Happily, this book came along before Brooke was too mature to go fishing with her silly old dad. I'm glad that she is only six, and that we can be taught to fish together by Phil Brunquell.

Tom Rosenbauer
East Arlington, Vermont

∾

ACKNOWLEDGMENTS

Foremost thanks go to my father, Philip Charles Brunquell, for his reassurance, and to my mother, Maria Antonia Brunquell, for her determination. The reference staff of the Welles-Turner Memorial Library in Glastonbury, Connecticut provided generous access to the fly-fishing literature, while my friend and secretary, Diane Pisani, patiently taught me how to process words. Medical photographers Michael McCarter and Joseph Driscoll paused graciously from their usual obligations to focus their cameras on the angler's world. Steve Balcanoff and Don Chaffee continue to offer invaluable on-site support to the fly-tying program at the Newington Children's Hospital. For their abiding interest in my children and others who have come to participate in their outstanding environmental programs, I am grateful to Carrol Adolph, Eleanor Thompson, and the instructors of the Catskill Fly Fishing Center. Carl Taylor, editor in chief of The Countryman Press, made this, my first foray into nonmedical publishing, a delight. And special gratitude is extended to the members of the Connecticut Fly Fishermen's Association for their wit, inspiration, and companionship.

PREFACE

Teaching children to fly-fish is like trying to mix oil and water. Fly-fishing demands attention to detail, freedom from both distractibility and impulsiveness, a high tolerance for frustration, and lots of patience. Every parent knows that children, effervescent and adorable though they are, do not instinctively major in these areas. But even oil and water can be made to mix if you add a little soap. This book is intended to be the soap.

Why bother working up a lather about fly-fishing? There are multiple answers, both universal and personal. Psychologists tell us that man's fascination with water stems from a desire to return to his embryonic beginnings, when he was immersed in the amniotic fluid. If this is true, and I believe it is, children's hold on things aquatic must be more tenacious than ours, because they are so much closer to their beginnings. Although this primordial urge can be satisfied in many ways, none is more enduring than fly-fishing. In later years, long after they've lost the ability to execute a high dive or score goals in water sports, the challenge of fly-fishing will remain accessible to them.

More immediate than this is the issue that forms the basis of just about every treatise on child rearing: communication. The barriers to communication with children are formidable, be they electronic (television and video games), temporal (incongruous work and school schedules), cognitive (kids don't understand why *New Yorker* cartoons are funny), or physical (you're stronger and more dexterous than your kids until a vaguely defined point in their adolescence when a mysterious reversal occurs).

Fly-fishing is an outstanding means of transcending these barriers. On the water, the myriad distractions and diversions that beseige the family are at least temporarily suspended. And, between the shared congratulations over fishes landed and the mutual condolences over fishes lost, there can emerge a common ground of appreciation and understanding.

The need for attentiveness and patience does not imply that fly-fishing is dry and regimented as, say, accounting. There is, after all, the heart-quickening moment when the strike is felt and the unbridled joy of skillfully handling the throbbing rod as the fish is brought to net. But to achieve this state of grace without some preliminary preparations is, for children as for adults, well-nigh impossible. A skeptic might argue that if parents are experienced, children will absorb fly-fishing skills by osmosis. Maybe, but that is a big maybe. I was not accomplished at the sport when the time was right for my kids to learn, and I presume there are many others like me. Even if I had been a fly-fishing expert, this would not have guaranteed that I'd know the best ways to convey the information to my children. What followed my own initiation to the sport was a lengthy series of trials and errors while fishing with my children, extensive reading after they were put to bed, and intensive discussions with other fly-fishing parents. The distillation of these experiences is what follows. I hope this soap forms a good emulsion.

———————————

P.B.

C H A P T E R   O N E

ORIENTATION

I firmly believe that the most ardent anglers harbor some hidden, profound grief. Fishing offers a recompense for their unhappiness and a release from the unremitting twin onslaughts of work and responsibility. This does not presuppose that such anglers need be as proficient as they are arduous. They may be, to put it bluntly, the clumsiest casters in the pool, but this does not faze them in the slightest, for they are there out of a need, a need for absolution and rebirth.

I doubt very much that kids look upon fishing this same way. They're out for fun and more specifically, immediate gratification. A feisty bluegill or perch (dare I say trout?) skittering at the end of their line can deliver what they're looking for. If you can direct them to this pleasure, if they see you as the one responsible for it, and if they learn some personal responsibility and environmental awareness along the way, then the entire family reaps the reward.

Of course, there are some obstacles that need to be overcome before this idyllic state can be reached. To start with, the child must have at least a modicum of interest. This might be difficult to muster with distractions such as high-tech video games competing for their attention. Fortunately, the trappings of fly-fishing are so mysterious and intriguing that it is difficult for a youngster to resist becoming at least a little inquisitive as a parent sorts through those arcane and colorful flies in preparation for yet another fishing trip.

Next, there is a minimum amount of critical information to master. If the kids are made to feel like they are sitting for the bar exam, a disappointing outcome is predictable. For whether you are casting to a wary brown or pitching the principles of the sport to your kids, presentation is paramount.

There is an overriding concern for safety, a topic that will be addressed extensively in these pages. Let's face it, having a sharp hook whizzing about the head of a child is unnerving at first, but with proper preparation and planning, a happy and safe time is attainable. And what about tackle selection? With rare exception, fly-fishing gear is not primarily designed with children in mind and yet with some simple modifications the problem can be surmounted.

Speaking of problems, one cannot ignore cost. Fly-fishing does not come cheap but there are many ways to save money, not the least of which is to avoid unnecessary purchases. I suspect you know what I mean. Open up your tackle box and count how many gadgets you've bought and don't use. See? At any rate, we'll talk about what I believe is the most economical way to go about outfitting a child for fly-fishing.

The gear, however, is not enough. You want your kids to learn the very best techniques, but what if you're no Charles Ritz? And aren't those fly-fishing schools mainly for adults and terribly expensive? Fortunately, there's also a way out of this one.

A final problem, and perhaps the most foreboding, is time. How does one make the time to do all of this? Believe me, I've wrestled with this one in a big way. As a physician, I have precious little discretionary time. How scheduling and prioritizing can assist in the conquest of this monster will repeatedly merit our attention.

℘

At what age should a child begin to fly-fish? This question has no easy answer. Conventional wisdom holds that fly-fishing is a rarified realm that one aspires to only after an assiduous apprenticeship with either cane pole or spinning rod. Implicit is the belief that it demands the hand and eye of the seasoned practitioner, one who has already drunk deeply of the vicissitudes of the sporting life.

This type of thinking does not seem to leave much room for children, so let's dispense with it right now without ignoring the very real restrictions imposed by age. In my professional life I've learned that at any given age children differ widely in their abilities and, therefore, selecting a single age when all children can legitimately adopt the sport is impossible. There are two essential requirements: The child must have the modicum of visual-motor skills necessary to lay out a fly line and also the judgment to avoid hazardous conditions when on the water. Perhaps because of these necessities, fly-fishing is often deferred until the child has reached mid- to late adolescence. This book's major premise is that for many children this delay is unnecessary, *provided they are placed in a consistently safe and supportive environment in which to develop their skills.* Given these circumstances, most children by the age of ten, and many by the age of eight, can learn to handle a fly rod with authority and satisfaction. Interestingly, strength is probably one of the least important requirements. With today's ultralight freshwater tackle, moving a lot of weight is not a factor, and the angular momentum provided by the relatively long fly rod enables the child, like the adult, to generate fast line speeds with relatively little movement of the casting arm.

I've made a number of assumptions in this book, and some explanation of them is in order. First, I've assumed that you are a parent and you are about to teach your son or daughter. This was done for two reasons: ease of exposition and because this role is a comfortable one for me, since it is the one I have occupied and continue to live through. The principles contained herein can be just as easily transmitted by other individuals, such as relatives, teachers, scout leaders, and camp instructors. I've also presupposed that your students are, like mine, between seven and fourteen years old. With little modification, the same principles can be offered to older adolescents and even veteran anglers may pick up a point or two in these pages.

When I refer to fly-fishing, I'm speaking about the freshwater variety. Not that I have anything against saltwater fly-rodding; on the contrary, I love it. Lou Tabory and Lefty Kreh's books sit on my nightstand as I write. But saltwater tackle is heavier and, hence, harder for children to handle, and saltwater fly-rodding generally places children in potentially riskier situations. So, if there are no strenuous objections, let's save the salt for a later time.

A final assumption is that you, the teacher, already have some grounding in the fundamentals of fly-fishing. If you don't, there is no reason to forsake this book. I've adopted this position because I did not wish to needlessly repeat what has already been presented elsewhere, both in print and video, by legions of highly capable and articulate sportsmen. Hence, we will not discuss the finer points of casting, reading the water,

Happiness is catching a handsome perch on a barbless Woolly Worm. The fish was quickly released after this picture was taken.

or matching the hatch. Instead, we will concentrate on the best means of conveying this information to your child. I learned fly-fishing in tandem with my children, so I know it can be done. If you are in need of the fundamentals, get a copy of Tom Rosenbauer's *The Orvis Fly-Fishing Guide* (Lyons and Burford, New York, 1984). This is one of the finest introductory texts available. And you might consider taking a fly-fishing course on your own. Then use this book to help channel all the wonderful information you've learned to your kids.

One of the really encouraging aspects of teaching children to fly-fish is that they tend to pick it up much more quickly than novice adults. This should come as no surprise, as they perform similarly in other areas. For example, kids learn foreign languages more quickly than adults. Their minds are not filled up with all the claptrap that adults carry around, such as who won the World Series in 1967. Thus they are free to seize upon new information with unrestrained relish. It's up to us, however, to make this introduction to the sport as attractive and safe as possible.

Will our efforts be premature? Shouldn't we just wait until the tykes have grown up to become investment bankers and lawyers when they will come across an exclusive tackle catalogue in someone's office and all will be revealed to them? The answer to these questions most certainly is *no*. The children's need for our attention is now. So is their need to be presented with alternatives to drug use, idleness, and what has been disturbingly called recreational violence. In addition, fly-fishing embodies a sense of conservationism and environmentalism that is sadly lacking in other forms of angling. We need to raise children who will help us reverse the destruction of natural resources for which our generation has largely been responsible.

Authorities tell us that fly-fishing is the most enjoyable form of angling because it places the fisherman in the closest, most direct contact with his quarry. In the following pages, I hope to show you how it can place you in direct contact with your children.

CHAPTER TWO

TACKLE TIME

THE FLY ROD

Giving your child her first fly rod is like giving her the keys to the family car for the first time: You're pleased that she has reached this state of readiness but are more than a little apprehensive about what comes next. Perhaps the easiest way to get her a rod is to give her one of yours. Unfortunately, this can turn out to be a very expensive proposition. The sequence goes like this: She gets the rod and is delighted. You smile. Soon the smile fades. You are looking at your rod rack and notice the vacancy. Initially, you are vaguely aware of a notion in your mind that the vacancy should be filled. The notion turns to desire and the desire grows to obsession. Suddenly, you're not sleeping at night, you're tired during the day, and your grouchiness hits stratospheric limits. The pressure builds until you feel as if you will burst. With abandon you rush out and plunk down the next two months' rent on a sweet piece of Tonkin fitted with nickel silver. There is momentary solace, a reprieve. Then, surely as winter follows autumn, you are swept away by buyer's remorse, coupled with an eroding sense of guilt that you did not really give your daughter your rod for her sake; it was purely a rationalization to justify your own gross consumerism and self-indulgence. You cad.

Take it from a cad who knows and save yourself from this shameful series of events. Be happy with your existing tackle. It has served you well and with the proper care you're giving it, will continue to do so. Besides, if you give her your rod and she breaks it, despite your external protestations, you will always internally feel that she broke *your* rod. Go out and get her something that is truly her own and has come as straight from your heart as from your wallet.

And what should that something be? First of all, resist fiberglass. The low cost of a glass rod will hit your brain like the sweet perfume of an evil temptress. You've seen such rods hanging by the hundreds in plastic blister packs at your local department store. Although such rods were the state of the art when we were kids, they just can't compare with graphite. The cost of graphite has come down since its introduction in the 70s. Now the price differential between a glass rod and a low-end graphite model is almost negligible. When you buy one, insist on at least 96 percent graphite, not those composite jobs that contain mostly glass with a smidgen of graphite thrown in just so the manufacturer can put the word graphite on the label. If the salesperson cannot tell you the percent of graphite composition by checking the manufacturer's specifications, walk away.

Another thing you should resist is a short rod. By short I mean anything less than eight feet. Many reputable manufacturers of fine tackle sell youth outfits that contain short rods. Maybe they think small hands need small rods. I think this is crazy. With the advent of ultralight graphite materials, the weight difference between a long and short rod designed for a given line size is not worth losing any sleep over. A large rod will do a better job of enabling the child to lift the line off the water and, more importantly, the longer length will keep the fly farther away from the child's head and body. I've not found the cork grips on longer rods to be too large for my children's hands, but Christopher and Amy are big for their ages. If your child's hands are small, a local rod maker should be able to sand down the grip for a nominal fee. Unless you are an experienced craftsman, do not take on this job yourself.

Every expert says never buy a rod that you haven't personally casted. Now this may make sense if you've had fly-fishing experience but if the rod is for your daughter and she's never casted before, telling the salesman to rig up the rod so she can try it right there can lead to interesting results, one of which is that your daughter will never speak to you again. However, don't think that just because you're genetically related to her, the rod will feel right in her hands if it feels right in yours.

In this situation, the best solution is for you to test the rod's action. This is a simple maneuver and nobody gets embarrassed. Grip the rod in the usual manner and extend it horizontally in front of you. Now briskly wag it back and forth. Fast-action rods flex mainly at the tip, medium-action rods bend down to the midsection, and slow-action rods flex all the way down to the butt. For children, I strongly recommend a slow-action rod. There are a number of reasons for this. The first is that when casting they are, well, slow. Using a slow-action rod means that the child's reactions do not have to be as quick or refined as when casting a stiffer model. It also means that there is more time to recognize casting errors and to correct them while the line and fly are still in the air. Slow rods enable the caster to feel the rod load and unload during the back and forward cast; fast-action rods inhibit this. Slow rods are especially suited for turning over wind-resistant flies such as the poppers and hair bugs designed for the child's most likely quarry, panfish. When it comes time to cast smaller flies to more selective fish like trout, the slow rod permits a more delicate presentation. Finally, casting a slow-action rod is so much more graceful and pleasing than wielding a stiffer stick. Watch your child casting and see what I mean. You can just imagine Robert Redford at your side, filming your child in slow motion for his next magnum opus.

Given these attributes, you might ask why every fly-fisher is not using a slow-action rod. What a slow-action rod lacks is the rigidity to propel the line great distances, and this is why it has fallen out of favor with many adult anglers, especially the macho types. By and large, children won't care a hoot about this factor, nor should adults. The majority of fish in fresh water will be caught within 20 feet of where you're standing anyway. For the average caster, a slow-action rod can perform nicely at twice this distance.

If these reasons still don't convince you that a slow-action, graphite rod is right for your child, consider this: For years, bamboo aficionados have been saying that graphite lovers are missing out on something incredible. If you've ever had the opportunity to cast a well-made cane rod, you'll know exactly what they mean. What is the major casting difference between bamboo and most graphite rods? The former are almost all slow action! It therefore follows that getting a well-made, slow-action graphite rod is the closest anyone can come to the feel of casting a fine piece of Tonkin—without paying a king's ransom.

The soft-action approach has its limits. You don't want your child wielding a wet noodle that puts excessive vibrations in the line and sends it nowhere. To avoid purchasing a rod like this, go back to the action test described above. As you are wagging the rod back and forth and it is flexing from tip to butt, suddenly stop. The rod should oscillate once or twice and then come to rest. If it doesn't, you've got a noodle in your hands, so pass it up.

JOSEPH DRISCOLL PHOTO

Fig. 2.1. Left: The rod sections are inserted into the rod bag with the ferrule ends facing downward. Right: When inserting the rod into the tube, the fingers of one hand encircle the tube opening to prevent damage to the guides.

The rod should be designed for a 6-weight line. This is perfect for young hands. Rods built for lighter line weights are more difficult to control and rods for heavier line weights are more likely to tire the child. The 6-weight will also handle the largest number of species your child is likely to encounter, from bluegill through trout to small bass.

When you buy a rod, be sure to pick up a rod bag and tube at the same time. There is an unwritten rule in fly-fishing that the longer the interval between buying the rod and purchasing the tube, the more likely the rod is going to be broken by the time it's first put in the tube. Although aluminum tubes are traditional, the Orvis Green Mountain tube is made of high-impact plastic, is cheaper, and has a D-shaped circumference so it won't roll around in the trunk of your car. Be sure to show your kids the proper way of inserting the rod in the tube (keep the ferrules down and encircle the opening of the tube with your fingers to avoid tearing off a guide on the edge of the tube—fig. 2.1).

REEL, BACKING, LINE, AND LEADER

There are no startling revelations here. The single-action reel with adjustable drag is standard. While we're on this subject, let me air one of my biggest gripes. Have you noticed that spinning reels are a whole lot cheaper than fly reels but the spinning reels have so many more parts? I guess this is because the tackle manufacturers believe all fly-fishers are affluent and naive, which most are not. Hence I have made it my personal mission to try to find a low-priced fly reel that performs as well as the top-of-the-line models. My search always comes back to the same item—the Pfluger Model 1594 (fig. 2.2). Unlike the better known 1494, the 1594 has the advantages of rim control and a counterweighted spool for only a modest difference in price.

This reel is a terrific buy. Like Timex watches and membership in the American Automobile Association, it's too good to pass up. It is sturdy as a tank, which is good if kids are going to use it, and it has an irresistible feature. When you crank it, it makes a delightful "put-put" sound, kind of like a finely tuned sports car.

If your child is a right-handed caster, he should reel with his left hand and vice versa. Then, following a strike, he will not have to transfer the rod to the opposite hand if he wishes to play the fish from the reel. Switching hands offers an excellent opportunity for slack to develop in the line and hence for the fish to get away.

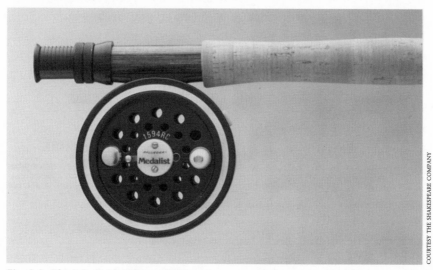

Fig. 2.2. The inimitable Pfluger 1594

Two admonitions about the 1594 are in order. Changing from right-to left-hand retrieve requires a degree in mechanical engineering and the patience to chase little parts that have fallen off the table and onto the floor. Have the tackle dealer do this for you. Second, buy a small screwdriver so you can keep the screws on the reel posts nice and snug.

Since most children begin fly-fishing in still waters where fish often lie deep, a slow-sinking line would seem a logical choice. I don't buy this. I believe it is better for a child to know where the line is at all times, so a weight-forward floating line is my preference. It's easier to pick up off the water, shoots better, and can always be used with a weighted leader or fly if there is a need to go deeper. Also, to aid visibility, select a bright color. I've never seen a fly line color stand out as much as fluorescent orange. Some authors make a big deal about using neutral or darker colors to avoid spooking fish. This is the purpose of the leader, not the line, so don't let their opinions sway you.

One way to save some cash when buying your child's first fly line is to select a shorter one. He's not going to start out by casting 80 feet anyway—and remember that most of the fish he'll catch will be within 20 to 30 feet of where he's standing. Scientific Anglers' Concept fly line is 57 feet long (most standard lines run 80 to 100 feet) and offers high quality at modest cost.

Do not expect your child to attach his leader to the fly line with a nail knot. You've heard about braided line-leader connectors? Well, you may curse as you try to get the thing on the end of the line, but once it's in place he'll thank you for it—and you'll be relieved he won't need your assistance every time he wants to change a leader. See chapter 3 for more about the connectors.

A word about backing. Everyone will tell you to put on enough backing so that the fly line comes to within one-fourth inch of the outside rim of the spool. This will keep your line from forming tight coils and will aid the speed of retrieval. For kids, I recommend you ignore this rule. Put on enough backing so that the line comes to within one-half inch of the outside rim. This way, there is less chance of loops of line falling astray when spools are changed, and there is less chance of line catching between the spool and the reel housing. Kids tend to go for flashy colors and now you can get fluorescent backing. Having fluorescent green backing attached to a fluorescent orange fly line in a black reel is, in my son's words, "truly maximum."

Leaders will be of the knotless tapered kind. If you think your child is going to sit there connecting lengths of different-sized monofilament with blood knots, you're dreaming. For now, tie a perfection loop at the butt end of his leader so he can make a loop-to-loop connection with the braided loop on his fly line. If you don't know how to tie a perfection loop, see chapter 3. Assuming your child will begin with bluegill, the only leader size you need is 3X. This will handle flies in size 8 through 12, which are just right for the little critters. Add a spool of 3X tippet material to keep the leader from disappearing and you're all set.

FLIES

Fly selection is determined by type of quarry. From my earlier comments you know I'm partial to kids beginning with panfish in general and bluegill in particular. This may seem self-evident, given that the bluegill's tendency to strike hard and often is perfectly matched to the child's relatively short attention span. But I have known purist parents who do not want their child to catch anything but a trout, believing that panfish are beneath the dignity of a fly-fisher. Given the difficulty in taking trout versus the child's inherent need for immediate gratification, this is a poor match. I'd rather spend an afternoon on a farm pond with my kids catching a mess of bluegills than fishing with them for a weekend on some storied trout water and catching nothing. Not that I can't tolerate being skunked. On the contrary, I'm an expert at it. But at this stage in their development, my children aren't.

If you carry the elitist attitude that panfish are trash fish, so will your children. The attitude is an entirely unnecessary one. I must admit that at one time I harbored a senseless guilt over enjoying these fish, but my subsequent readings told me that if some of the world's most accomplished anglers can wax poetic about them, so can I. Consider the following:

> In 49 of our 50 states warm- and cool-water panfish are more widespread in distribution and eager to bite than trout or bass. And there's so much more to catching them than you might imagine. So this feature speaks to every fly-fisher about catching these pan-size critters and not as just a prelude to catching other, bigger fish. Maybe it's time you come back to panfish if the fast-lane adult life and the high pressure of Atlantic salmon, bonefish, or tournament fishing have you down. With a fresh perspective and a challenging

approach, panfish can open a new future of fly-fishing pleasure for you. You might just rediscover what attracted you to the sport in the first place. And if you're just getting started, panfishing is the place to learn quickly and enjoyably the techniques that you will use for other fly-rod species. Panfish have provided me with some of my most enjoyable moments in fly-fishing.

Dave Whitlock, "Panfish, Parts I and II,"
Fly Fisherman, 22(5), May and July 1991

Or how about:

...I do believe it's time that we gave the bluegill his proper due.

I'm not talking about those stunted little specimens the size of a Ritz cracker that we all caught as kids, and that have given the bluegill a bad name among serious anglers. The bluegills I fish for weigh close to a pound and are bigger than my hand. On light tackle they put a bend in my rod and a cramp in my wrist. Moreover, bluegill fillets, dipped in milk, rolled in crumbled cornflakes, and fried in butter make the sweetest eating of all freshwater fish. Personal opinion.

William G. Tapply
Those Hours Spent Outdoors: Reflections on Hunting and Fishing
Charles Scribner's Sons, New York, 1988

And if there are any of you who think going for panfish is too simple to be interesting, read this:

My friends and I will usually show up at a farm pond all decked out for high sport with neoprene waders, belly boats, fly rods, cameras: the whole thing. We remember when it was different, but this is just how we do it now. We have become fly-fishermen.

Between us we carry fly patterns that imitate just about any warmwater food organism you can name, plus those goofy things that have what pass for anatomical features, but that nonetheless look like nothing nature has ever produced on this planet. After all, fish don't think like we do.

Sometimes we'll take the temperature of the water, someone

---

usually knows what the barometer is doing at the moment and there may be talk of water chemistry, aquatic vegetation, moon phase, photo-periods as they relate to spawning and feeding activity, insect migration patterns and so on.

Now and then the owner of the pond will be impressed. More likely he'll be amused and a little puzzled, wondering how we got it into our heads that anything, let alone fishing, was that complicated.

John Gierach, *Even Brook Trout Get the Blues*
Simon and Schuster, New York, 1992.
Reprinted by permission of Knox Burger Associates, Ltd.

Selecting flies for panfish may seem like a contradiction in terms, since panfish by nature are not very selective. Nonetheless, they are not easy to take on *every* outing, and there are patterns that are consistently more productive than others. Our family's top ten are shown in fig. 2.3 and some of the dressings are given in appendix B. Like most other species, panfish do most of their feeding under the surface, so we are partial to wet flies, particularly those that are yellow (like the McGinty) or white (such as the White Miller).

Panfishing has several close parallels to fly-rodding for trout, not the least of which is that taking them on the surface is the most challenging as well as the most fun. Although dry flies will occasionally work, the Adams of panfishing is the small (size 8 to 12) popper. If you really want to hear your kids scream with delight, have them experience a bluegill smashing onto a popper which they are chugging along the surface of the water. It will be one of their most memorable angling experiences, as well as one of yours.

THE "S" WORD

A not uncommon scenario is that a parent desperately wants his child to fly-fish and although the child wants to do the same, her coordination just isn't there. Since tying some of the simpler fly patterns is actually easier than casting, the parent may be faced with the paradox that the child can tie a fly but not cast it. Fortunately, this need not signify a halt in the youngster's angling development. All you need to do is take a deep breath, screw up your courage, forget all the disparaging remarks you've

JOSEPH DRISCOLL PHOTO

Fig. 2.3. Patterns for panfish. Clockwise from top: Cork-Bodied Popper, McGinty, Woolly Worm, Joe's Hopper, Rio Grande King, Girdle Bug, White Miller, Muddler Minnow, Foam-Bodied Spider, Gold-Ribbed Hare's Ear Nymph. All flies tied by the author.

heard among your buddies, and muster the "S" word: spin-casting.

Now if you are a fly-fishing purist, and a dry-fly angler in particular, you've probably just popped a cork. But calm down and let's get real: It's your child's happiness that's on the line. And fly rod or no fly rod, the thrill of catching a fish on a fly she tied herself will certainly be one of her happiest moments.

The closed-face, button-operated bail makes the spin-casting outfit the easiest type of tackle to cast on this planet. It is orders of magnitude easier than using a fly rod and significantly easier than the traditional open-faced spinning reel. As spin-casting outfits require weighted lures to carry out the line and flies are essentially weightless, one must either add split shot to the leader (use the nonleaded kind) or use a casting bubble. Most aficionados prefer the latter.

Casting bubbles differ from the usual bobbers in that the line passes through the center of the bubble rather than being attached to its outer surface, and bubbles allow various amounts of water to enter their interiors to supply the weight necessary to cast the fly.

By far the easiest bubble to use is the A-JUST-A-BUBBLE (fig. 2.4). There's no need to deal with swivels or complicated knots. The A-JUST-A-BUBBLE comes in four sizes: one-eighth, three-sixteenths, one-fourth, and three-eighths ounce. Choose the one that's right for your spinning rod (spinning rods are sized for particular weight lures the way fly rods are sized for different weight fly lines).

Here's how to rig up. Pass the monofilament line through the bubble with the wide end of the bubble toward the fly end of the line. Now grab the knob on the wide end and rotate the bubble. This will twist

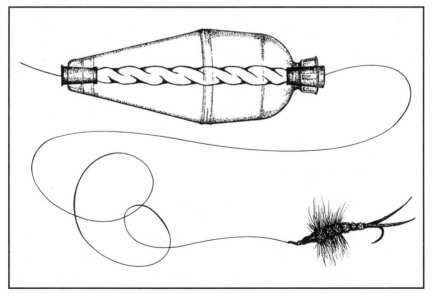

Fig. 2.4. The A-JUST-A-BUBBLE. The wide end faces the fly. Rotating the outer casing causes an internal rubber tube to twist and fix the position of the bubble on the line.

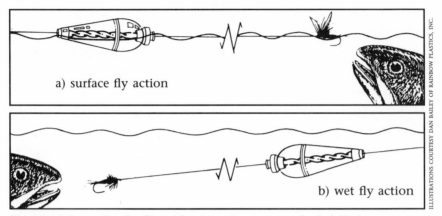

Fig. 2.5. a) For casting dry flies with spin-casting gear, use the "mini" size A-JUST-A-BUBBLE with two- to four-lb.-test line. Fill the bubble with just enough water to cast beyond the rising fish. b) For streamers, wet flies, and nymphs, place the A-JUST-A-BUBBLE about four feet in front of the fly and fill with sufficient water to maintain neutral buoyancy.

the rubber tube on the inside of the bubble and fix it into position. To admit water into the bubble, simply hold it firmly in one hand and pull the knob out with the other. Once you've filled the bubble with the desired amount of water, relax your hold on the knob so that it reseats itself into position, thus trapping the water inside. By regulating the amount of water entering the bubble, your child will be able to fish at different depths (fig. 2.5).

A-JUST-A-BUBBLE is available in the U.S. from Rainbow Plastics, Inc., P.O. Box 1861, Fort Collins, Colorado 80522 and in Canada from either Western Canada Importers, 1825-30 Avenue NE, Calgary, Alberta T2P 2J6 or Redl Sports Distributor, 7590 Conrad Street, Burnaby, British Columbia V5A 2H7.

CAPS AND GLASSES

The fishing cap has many purposes. Your child can imitate the famous Montana guides by brazenly tossing the cap on the ground and putting the butt section of the rod into the cap's interior to protect the reel from dirt while rigging up. The cap can be a source of self-expression if he is allowed to decorate it with patches and logo pins of his own choosing. And most importantly, the cap helps to protect his face and head from the sun and the fly.

Although an ordinary baseball cap will do, the best type is the fore-and-aft version that comes with a rear flap to protect the ears (fig. 2.6). The front visors on the good models have a soft green underlining to reduce glare. Kids seem to be more sensitive than adults to the fact that these hats look, well, unconventional, and so they may be less inclined to wear them. Here's where bribing them with patches and logo pins may induce compliance.

Ideally the sunglasses you get for your child should be polarized.

Fig. 2.6. The fore-and-aft cap and sunglasses with built-in side shields offer protection from the sun, insects, and the fly.

Fig. 2.7. Both the clear-lensed (left) and tinted (right) versions of children's eyewear offered by the Cabot Safety Corporation provide UV protection, built-in side shields, and attractive design at low cost.

Folks will tell you that polarized lenses will cut glare from the water's surface and allow you to spot fish. This is true, but I view their main advantage as a means of avoiding a dunking because my kids are able to spot holes and drop-offs when wading. Trying to find an inexpensive pair of polarized sunglasses for your children can be a real challenge. The types sold on racks in most tackle stores are too large to fit most children comfortably.

Insist on lenses with ultraviolet (UV) protection. Sunglasses without such protection are an unfortunate combination: The dark lenses will cause your child's pupils to dilate, thus admitting more of the sun's damaging UV rays to the interior of the eye. Also, insist on built-in side shields. These are necessary not only to reduce glare but also to protect your child's eyes should an ill-placed cast or the wind send the fly toward him from the side.

A source of attractive, inexpensive sunglasses with UV protection and side shields is the Cabot Safety Corporation (90 Mechanic Street, Southbridge, Massachusetts 01550 or 7115 Tomken Road, Mississauga,

Ontario, Canada L5S 1R8). Their Aerosite Jelly Bean and Aerosite Neons Safety Eyewear come in kids' sizes and attractive colors such as cranberry red, blueberry blue, beach plum purple, and "collage" tricolored frames (fig. 2.7). You will find that these models have a high rate of acceptance among kids. Unfortunately, the lenses are not polarized. My search for a pair of glasses that has all of the wonderful Cabot features including low cost but with polarized lenses continues as of this writing.

One problem with sunglasses is that they lead to eyestrain during low light conditions, as on overcast days and during the early morning or evening hours. During the warmer months, these are precisely the times when fish are most likely to bite. Fortunately, there is no need to lay down the rod for lack of protective eyewear on these occasions. The Cabot Safety Corporation also makes clear-lens models of their safety glasses for children (fig. 2.7) and these have UV protection.

Getting kids to wear cap and glasses on the water is much like getting them to wear seat belts in the car: They are more likely to do it if you do it. Pediatricians tell families that children should learn from an early age that the car simply does not move unless everyone's seat belts are fastened. Similarly, your kids should know that no cast is made until the caps and glasses are on.

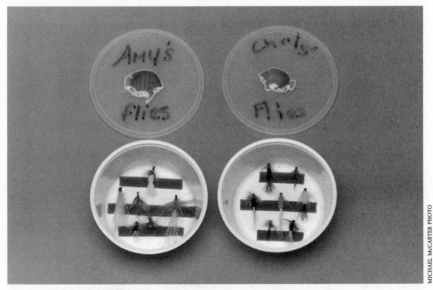

Fig. 2.8. The margarine tub as fly box. All flies tied by the children.

WHAT YOUR CHILD DOESN'T NEED

Many of you may object to some of the items on this list. My only defense is that the list reflects my personal biases and my children have missed none of this stuff, particularly since low-cost substitutions are readily available.

WHEATLEY FLY BOX: Recycled plastic margarine tubs can fulfill the same purpose, albeit with less aplomb. Pieces of self-adhesive open-cell poly foam weatherstripping (such as Ace Hardware Weatherizer number 51272) can be applied to the tub's interior to hold the flies. Also, your kids can decorate the tubs using colorful stickers and markers (fig. 2.8), something you *don't* want them doing to a Wheatley fly box.

    If you eventually do spring for a real fly box, my recommendation is the Scientific Anglers System model (fig. 2.9). The interior is made of open- rather than closed-cell foam, so it doesn't crumble into tiny bits when you extract a fly. The box floats and the inserts are replaceable. Don't get the small size even though it looks cute. Once your kids start tying, they'll appreciate the roominess of the medium or large box.

REEL CASE: Just insert the reel inside an old, clean athletic sock and seal with a rubber band.

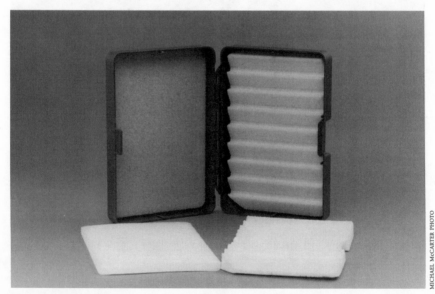

Fig. 2.9. Scientific Anglers' System fly box with removable inserts.

FISHING VEST: If you must spring for this, fine. Or, you can go to an army & navy store and pick up one of those army shirts with all the deep pockets, size small. If your child wades, however, a PFD (Personal Flotation Device) is mandatory (see chapter 5).

ZINGER: Sew a strip of elastic to the army shirt; it will last eons longer than a zinger.

CLIPPER WITH RETRACTABLE PIN: Ordinary nail clippers from your bathroom cabinet will do. Attach to the end of the elastic strip; then take a safety pin and insert it through the buttonhole of one of the pocket flaps on the shirt.

FLY PATCH: A wine cork connected to another short strip of elastic that is sewn onto the shirt will do nicely.

KNOT TOOLS: Ugh! See chapter 3 for further explanation. Substitution: your fingers.

WADERS: Forget 'em. Have the kids wade wet, but only when air and water temperatures permit.

WADING BOOTS: For slippery surfaces, have them wear old pairs of high-topped sneakers to which you've glued felt soles (sold as replacements at fly shops) with Barge cement.

LANDING NET: Teach them to wet their hands before they pick up fish and also what parts of which fish not to touch.

TIPPET DISPENSERS: All you need is one spool of 3X, so why bother with a dispenser?

CREEL: Perish the thought. We're talking catch-and-release, right?

LINE LUBRICANT AND PROTECTANT: Substitute Armor All, available in any hardware store. One container will last generations.

LEATHER-BOUND FIELD JOURNAL: Skip it and buy a pocket pad from K Mart.

TINY POCKET SEINES: Give me a break. When you seine with your kids, you want to seine Texas style! See chapter 6.

LINE WINDER: This may be essential for the rich and famous but your kids and mine can live without it. When loading line onto a reel, sit down, insert an unsharpened pencil through the line spool, cradle the pencil between the insides of your knees, and wind the line onto the reel through the stripping guide on your rod. When removing the line from the reel at the end of the season, wrap it loosely around an old coffee can and use twists of pipe cleaner to keep the coils from unwinding.

MONOFILAMENT WASTE WALLET: Simply tell your child to designate a pocket in his clothing for this purpose and remind him to dispose of the contents properly when he gets home.

BEFRIENDING THE TACKLE

Once your child has acquired the necessary equipment, he'll need to become thoroughly familiar with it. This is not necessarily a simple task. Remember when you opened a fly-tackle catalogue for the first time and how confusing all the paraphernalia seemed? Kids will not acquire this fund of knowledge in an evening nor are they likely to engage in the prolonged tackle musings that adult anglers revel in. One successful method of getting the information across is to meter it out in small doses when they are a captive audience, such as riding with you in the car. I devised a series of "road quizzes" which I gave them once when we took a long car trip to some distant waters (see appendix A). They loved the challenge, particularly since it gave them yet another opportunity to compete with one another. Each quiz is brief, so the testing can be easily terminated if their interest flags and then taken up again at another time. The quizzes are also arranged in order of increasing complexity. Don't be surprised if your child says, "This is a cinch" after the first one but is clamoring for assistance later on. This latter situation is, of course, what trouty parents love, because then at least you have your foot in the door to give them some firsthand information, however briefly their attention may last.

Recently I've expanded the quizzes to include topics such as stream entomology and water ecology; all of this will connect with chapters 6 and 10.

LOSS OF GEAR

Since children have a tendency to lose things, make sure their tackle is labeled. Here is yet another reason to get involved with Trout Unlimited (for the main reasons, see chapter 7). TU offers its contributors address labels with attractive catch-and-release logos on them. I've put the labels on all of our fly and tackle boxes as well as on our first-aid kit. Overlying the labels with clear plastic tape and covering the tape with a thin coat of paste wax will help prevent moisture from ruining the labels.

It helps if your child's fishing hat has one of those special lanyards with clips on both ends. One clip attaches to the rear brim of her hat while the other attaches to the back of her shirt collar. If a stiff breeze comes along, the hat will not be history. Similarly, an eyeglass lanyard is a good idea. Get the longer kind so that the glasses are not held tightly against her face; the short models are cumbersome to remove. With the looser kind, she can easily take off the glasses when necessary and just let them dangle in front, rather than putting them down on the bank and forgetting them.

Consider designating one person as the supply master for the group. Initially this will be you. Carry one set of clippers, one box of flies, and so on, so there is less likelihood of loss. As your children's skills and responsibility develop, this function can gradually be transferred to them. In recognition of their responsible behavior you may wish to reward them with their own set of clippers or other such item.

C H A P T E R   T H R E E

KNOTS? NOT!

I remember the first time I took my dad to watch some fly-fishing. The sport was foreign to him, for he had been devoted exclusively to spin-casting with bait and plugs for over 65 years. We went to the Junction Pool on the Beaverkill River. A caddis hatch was on, so there were plenty of anglers in evidence. It was a perfect day: The sky was clear, the fish were rising, and most of the anglers were connecting. I was pleased that Dad could see fly-fishing in all of its glory. After a lengthy period of observation, I turned to him and said, "Well, Dad, what do you think?" He looked at me and said dryly, "Those fishermen are spending an awful lot of time tying knots."

It's true. You can't become really fond of fly-fishing if you don't relish tying knots, and lots of them. This presents a major problem for kids. Although the image of the Boy Scout earning mounds of merit badges for his knot tying is both satisfying and idyllic, once you put a fly rod in his hand, he does not want to tie knots. He wants to catch fish.

If you refer to the standard fly-fishing texts, the problem seems insurmountable. There are knots designed for every conceivable fly-fishing situation. Mark Sosin and Lefty Kreh, in *Practical Fishing Knots II* (Lyons and Burford, New York, 1991), list over 40 varieties. One thing is certain. Knot-tying tools are not the answer. I own four different types, and I never use them. They don't always work, are sometimes expensive, and will reduce your children's self-reliance. If you insist on knot-tying tools, call me. I've been trying to unload mine for years and will give you a good price. There are two solutions to the knot problem that I can offer. The first is called nearly knotless fly-fishing and the second is knotless fly-fishing.

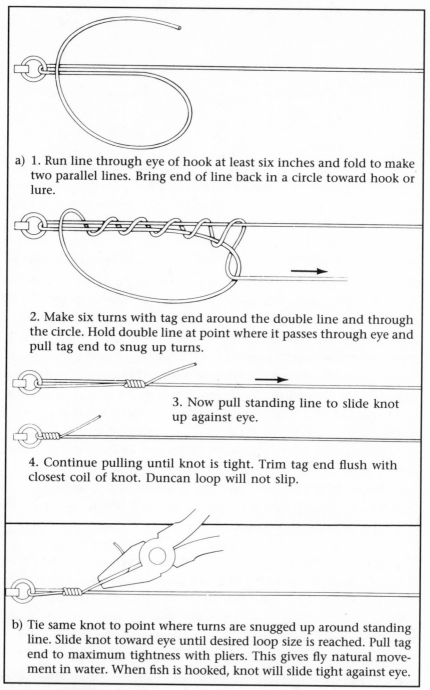

a) 1. Run line through eye of hook at least six inches and fold to make two parallel lines. Bring end of line back in a circle toward hook or lure.

2. Make six turns with tag end around the double line and through the circle. Hold double line at point where it passes through eye and pull tag end to snug up turns.

3. Now pull standing line to slide knot up against eye.

4. Continue pulling until knot is tight. Trim tag end flush with closest coil of knot. Duncan loop will not slip.

b) Tie same knot to point where turns are snugged up around standing line. Slide knot toward eye until desired loop size is reached. Pull tag end to maximum tightness with pliers. This gives fly natural movement in water. When fish is hooked, knot will slide tight against eye.

Fig. 3.1. Attaching fly to leader with the Duncan Loop: a) tight version;
b) open-looped version

NEARLY KNOTLESS FLY-FISHING

This method requires that the child know how to tie one and only one knot: the Duncan loop (figs. 3.1 and 3.2). You may object that this knot is too difficult for a child to master. If you stop and think about it however, tying your shoelaces involves a more complex series of steps. So if your youngster can tie her shoes, she can probably tie the Duncan loop.

This knot just about does it all. You can use it to tie backing to the reel, fly line to backing, leader to fly line, and fly to leader. The one area where this method falls a little short is the addition of tippet material to the leader. Although the Duncan loop will work here too, the double surgeon's knot (fig. 3.3) is easier. Or, if your child prefers to remain with the one-knot system, he can tie on a larger fly as the leader shortens with successive fly changes (panfish will generally not stop hitting if you go up a few fly sizes), or change the whole leader. Another possible adjustment to this system involves the braided loop connector discussed in chapter 2 (fig. 3.4). Here you can work out a division of labor with your child: You put the connector on the fly line and tie a perfection loop (fig. 3.5) on the butt end of the leader, while he learns to make the loop-to-loop connection between the two (fig. 3.6).

One of the real bugaboos children encounter when learning to fly-

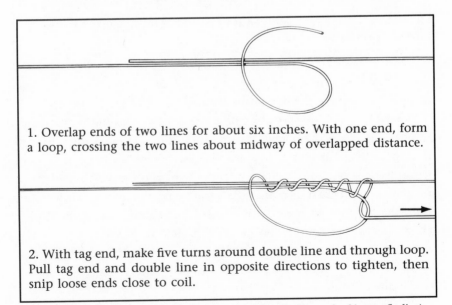

1. Overlap ends of two lines for about six inches. With one end, form a loop, crossing the two lines about midway of overlapped distance.

2. With tag end, make five turns around double line and through loop. Pull tag end and double line in opposite directions to tighten, then snip loose ends close to coil.

Fig. 3.2. Connecting two lines (for example, leader to fly line or backing to fly line) with the Duncan loop

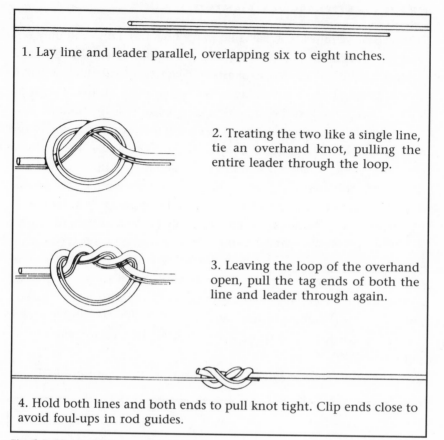

1. Lay line and leader parallel, overlapping six to eight inches.

2. Treating the two like a single line, tie an overhand knot, pulling the entire leader through the loop.

3. Leaving the loop of the overhand open, pull the tag ends of both the line and leader through again.

4. Hold both lines and both ends to pull knot tight. Clip ends close to avoid foul-ups in rod guides.

Fig. 3.3. The double surgeon's knot

fish is their yanking the line-leader connection through the tiptop when retrieving line. This is especially a problem if they've had prior experience spincasting, when the bobber hitting the tiptop reminded them to stop reeling in line. Now that they are fly-fishing sans bobber, the helpful reminder is gone. To overcome this problem, you can use one of those foam press-on strike indicators, but instead of putting it on the leader, put it on the fly line just behind the braided loop connector. Then, if your child attempts to strip in too much line, he'll have a visual as well as tactile clue to tell him to stop his retrieve. One problem with this method is that a sticky residue is left on the fly line once the strike indicator eventually falls off.

A different solution is to have your child make a cast and then retrieve line just to the point where enough line (about 15 to 20 feet) is out beyond the tiptop for another cast. At this point, mark the line where it rests beneath the index finger of her casting hand. Using a short length of monofilament, a Duncan loop is tied over the line at this spot. The ends are trimmed closely and the knot can be coated with some Pliobond. Now when she is retrieving line she will know to stop as soon as she feels the knot slide under her index finger.

KNOTLESS FLY-FISHING

This is a blatant contradiction, since everyone knows there can be no truly knotless fly-fishing. However, it can be *as far as the kids are concerned.* The trick, if you have not guessed already, is that you are the one tying the knots! But most emphatically, *this is not done on the water.* Imagine how long the kids' attention would last if you're up to your ears in nail knots while a hatch is on and the trout are gorging themselves.

All knot tying should be done at home. If we've got a Saturday fishing trip planned, it goes something like this. First, I put the kids to bed

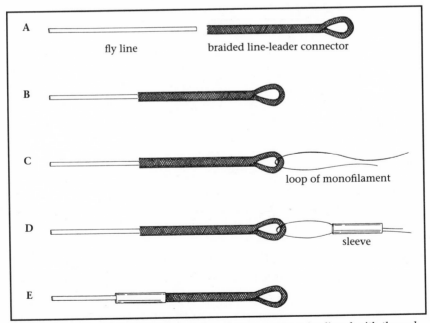

Fig. 3.4. The braided line-leader connector. a) The connector is aligned with the end of the fly line. b) The connector is inched over the line. c) A piece of monofilament is threaded through the braided loop. d) A plastic sleeve is passed over the ends of monofilament. e) The sleeve is slid over the junction of the fly line and the connector.

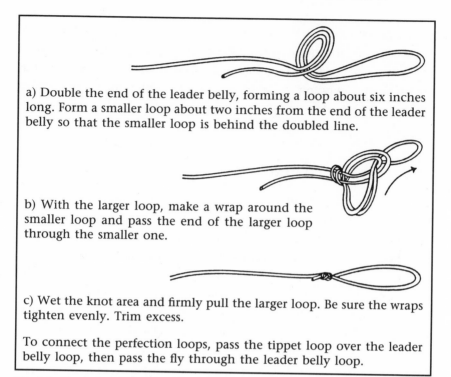

a) Double the end of the leader belly, forming a loop about six inches long. Form a smaller loop about two inches from the end of the leader belly so that the smaller loop is behind the doubled line.

b) With the larger loop, make a wrap around the smaller loop and pass the end of the larger loop through the smaller one.

c) Wet the knot area and firmly pull the larger loop. Be sure the wraps tighten evenly. Trim excess.

To connect the perfection loops, pass the tippet loop over the leader belly loop, then pass the fly through the leader belly loop.

Fig. 3.5. The perfection loop knot is used at the ends of the leader belly and the tippet.

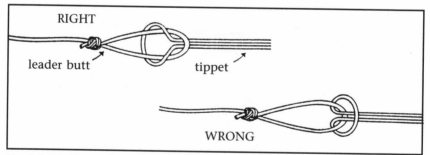

Fig. 3.6. The loop-to-loop connection

early Friday evening. Then I turn on National Public Radio, pour a small glass of wine, and get started. Flies are selected and each of them is snelled onto a length of monofilament. I use the Duncan loop to attach the fly to one end, and tie a perfection loop on the other (fig. 3.7). For panfish flies, short lengths of 3X tippet material do nicely, and the completed rigs are stored in one of those inexpensive snelled hook holders available in most tackle shops. Avoid the spring-loaded kind, as they may snap apart

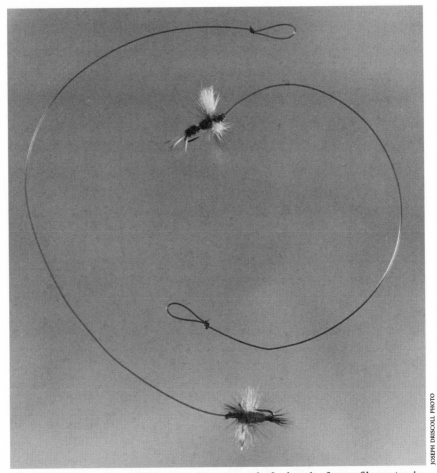

Fig. 3.7. A fly can be snelled by tying it to one end of a length of monofilament using a Duncan loop. A perfection loop on the opposite end permits attachment to the leader using a loop-to-loop connection.

the delicate tippets. I also make sure that perfection loops are tied at the end of their leaders. When we're on the water the next day, all they have to do is select a fly from the holder and loop-to-loop it onto the tippet end of the leader. If the fly breaks off, they just select another from the holder and repeat the process with no knots to worry about.

For trout flies, finer tippet material of longer lengths is generally required, making the snelled hook holder impractical. In this case, again use the Duncan loop to tie the fly onto either the tippet material or an entire leader, and secure a perfection loop on the opposite end. Attach the whole shebang to a homemade cast carrier. These are simple devices to

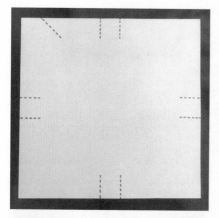

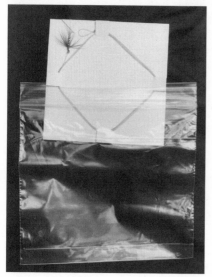

Fig. 3.8. The homemade cast carrier. Top left: Card with markings for slots. Top right: The carrier loaded with the leadered fly, ready to be inserted into the self-sealing plastic bag at left.

JOSEPH DRISCOLL PHOTOS

make; I first learned about them from an article written by Art Lee ("Wet Flies By The Cast," *Fly Fisherman*, March 1986, pp. 36–37). With slight adjustment to Mr. Lee's original method, here's how I do it (fig. 3.8):

Cut out a square of cardboard about the size of a slice of bread (4½ by 4½ inches). Now cut four tabs, one on each side of the square. Each tab should be centered around the middle of its respective side. Then make a single diagonal slot near the corner of just one of the sides. Take the snelled fly, and insert the bend of the hook into the slot. Guide the rest of the leader material around the four tabs until you get to the perfection loop. If you wish you can cut another slot in the edge of the cardboard at this spot to hold the loop. Finally, slide the carrier into one of those self-sealing clear plastic sandwich bags. Repeat this process until you have enough flies prepared for the following day.

If you'd prefer something more durable than cardboard, go for the Custom Caddy from Terminal Tactics, Inc. (432 Nanda Knoll, P.O. Box 455, Sauk Rapids, Minnesota 56379) or in Canada from Hook and Hackle Industries (P.O. Box 6, Lethbridge, Alberta T1J 3Y3). This item can be purchased empty or loaded with either trout or bass/panfish flies and matching color-coded leaders (fig. 3.9). Each caddy will hold two leadered flies, and two caddies slip into a plastic case that can be popped into your shirt pocket or attached to your vest with the supplied velcro material (fig. 3.10). Custom Caddies are also made for spin rod fly-fishing and come with those neat casting bubbles I talked about in chapter 2. My kids and I have used the Custom Caddies for two seasons now and love them. The beauty of these items is that you can fish all day and literally spend zero time tying knots while on the water.

The English have been using cast carriers for years, and why the message hasn't spread like wildfire across the Atlantic beats me. Although carriers were originally designed to store leaders with multiple droppers, I don't advise that children use such rigs. Droppers have a nasty habit of tangling around the leader and, quite frankly, one fly whizzing about is plenty for your youngster (and you) to keep track of.

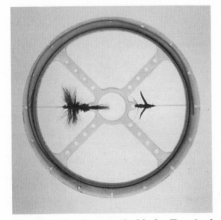

Fig. 3.9. The Custom Caddy by Terminal Tactics, Inc. is a durable means of storing leadered flies. Each caddy holds two rigs.

Fig. 3.10. Two Custom Caddies slip into a protective case bearing a color key that enables leader size to be recognized at a glance. The case can be carried in a vest pocket or attached to the vest exterior with supplied velcro material.

With the passage of time, it is expected that your children will gradually assume their own knot-tying responsibilities. I cannot in all fairness speak to this, for although my kids have mastered the Duncan loop and the loop-to-loop connection, they still manage to have me tie most of their knots!

CHAPTER FOUR

OUTINGS

When should you take your kids fly-fishing? Well, if you consult your almanac, you'll do it when the moon is between new and full, the tide is near peak or ebb, the barometer is rising and the wind is from the west. The day should be cloudy with a slight chop on the water so the fish won't see you, but not so windy that your line will foul. A blizzard hatch also helps.

Now all of this is fine if you are independently wealthy so you don't have to work, and the kids have dropped out of school. For the rest of us, as the saying goes, we fish when we can. Not that you should ignore these other things. Squinting up at the sky, checking the solunar tables, and tapping the barometer (even if you don't know how to read it) adds to the mystique of fly-fishing, and your kids may be coaxed into thinking you're some sort of Mark Trail, not an altogether unpleasant situation.

Once you're on the water together, a complex relationship develops, and it's good to consider ahead of time what direction you want it to take. For instance, think about guides. Have you ever used a guide, or know someone who has? Then you know that the good ones are patient, don't condescend, and never fish when their clients are doing so. Your kids are in the same position as the clients, and whether they realize it or not, their needs are the same. The cardinal difference is that the kids usually don't have a choice of which guide they'd like to be with! Whenever I'm out fishing with my children and things are threatening to take a sour turn, I stop and think about the guide analogy and usually act accordingly. More often than not, this sets things straight.

For many parents, not fishing while their kids are can be extremely frustrating, especially if there are plenty of rise forms in evidence. The way I see it, it's a trade-off. The earlier you devote yourself to being their guide, the sooner they will become independent so that you can fish equally together. If you insist on hogging the fishing for yourself, that point in time will only be pushed further into the future. It follows that separate times must be set aside to purge your own angling desires. Then, when you're astream with your kids, your thoughts will settle on their needs and not your own.

In this chapter I've conceived of fly-fishing instruction as occurring in a series of outings. These follow one another in a logical progression. Although the progression is not inviolable, it does impress upon the child that advanced skills require mastery of the fundamentals. By proposing this order, I do not imply that this is the only path to fly-fishing enlightenment, nor do I wish to rob you or your children of any of the spontaneity or surprise that learning the craft provides. I know that you will ad lib freely, and that once you are on the water there will be no lack of unexpected things to discover and show one another.

Not all of the outings actually involve fishing. This was intentional and is based upon the almost universal belief among fly-fishers that catching fish is a small, albeit very important part of the undertaking. This also explains why several other chapters in this book have nothing to do with laying a line on the water. These other activities are not extraneous; they can all be subsumed under what Dave Whitlock calls "the arts of fly-fishing."

The outings seek to subdivide the larger skills into smaller parts, so the child need not be overwhelmed by a sudden avalanche of new things to learn. Furthermore, each outing can be contracted or expanded according to the child's attention span on any particular day. Parts of different outings can be recombined to answer what is happening on the stream or pond when you chance to be there. Finally, there are no time limits. These outings can be done in a single season or dispersed over a lifetime.

FIRST ENCOUNTERS OF THE FINEST KIND

Do you remember the first time you went to a stream and saw someone fly-fishing? Did it have a profound effect upon you? If your answers to these questions are yes, then we have a lot in common. A few years ago, during a bitter cold February, I took the family to see the Farmington River. I was just becoming aware of fly-fishing at the time, and although I had glanced at some books and videos, I had never actually seen someone fly-fishing in the flesh, so to speak. Now I wasn't really expecting to see anyone on the water during that grim time of year, but I wanted to check out the river in all of its winter barrenness in order to figure out where I might start fishing the following spring.

We followed the river along a lovely road and ultimately pulled the car into the parking lot of a Methodist church. We walked across the road to get to the riverbank, and after climbing a small rise, we met an image that has never since left me. The water and sky were fused into a sheet of steely gray, the air was as still as a cathedral's, and emerging from the surface of the river were the spectral forms of half a dozen men, each gracefully casting his line in a silent, almost mystical ballet. One of the anglers, an older man, looked up, smiled, and quietly waved. My children gasped audibly, for they too were taken with the unexpected beauty of the scene.

I subsequently learned that this stretch of water is the celebrated Church Pool. Since the appearance of the fly rod in this country, there's been scarcely a picosecond that this pool hasn't been crawling with anglers. Had we been equipped with this foreknowledge, the scene may well have been robbed of its preternatural qualities, and I doubt that it would have left such an impression on us.

The whole point of this digression is that first impressions last, and if you wish to explore the possibility that your children might be interested in fly-fishing, the initial step is to refrain from going out and buying a high-modulus, high-priced, graphite fly rod. Rather, take them where they can observe others practicing the craft. You can then gauge their reaction and decide how, if at all, you wish to proceed. In our case, I was blessed. Both kids got so excited, they wanted me to immediately find a store where I would get them each a pair of waders so they could jump into the frigid waters along with the other anglers. Fortunately for my kids' safety, the integrity of my wallet, and the sanity of the fishermen, I did not oblige. The seed, however, was planted, so that by the following spring the kids were doing what every fly-fishing parent passionately prays for: It was they who were dragging me back to the river.

DAPPING, DUMPING, AND TROLL-WALKING

History tells us that all of civilization's successful and enduring move-ments, be they political, social, or religious, center about a basic theme or construct from which all other precepts are derived. For Hinduism it is the Doctrine of Reincarnation; for Christianity the Golden Rule; for the United States Government, the Constitution. And for fly-fishing, it is the Cast. It is fair to say that in fly-fishing circles, the status of the Cast has even preempted that of the Fish. For in every fly-fisher's mind, the Cast occu-pies approximately 96 percent of his mental life. The religion of the Cast has almost taken on a life of its own. Not only have volumes been written about it, but if you approach a cadre of fly-fishers discussing their exploits, chances are that they'll be talking more about their casting than whether anybody caught anything. Fortunately, this process has not advanced to the point that a rebellious sect of Pure Casters (*totally* cerebral fly-fishers) has broken off from the mainstream congregation. But if this ultimately happens, I won't be surprised. And if our rivers get any worse and all the trout die off, it may *have* to happen.

What does all of this have to do with kids? Well, it means that if we believe casting ability is a prerequisite for our youngsters' even thinking about approaching a body of water with fly rod in hand, we might all have a very long wait. Fortunately there are three maneuvers that can be quickly mastered while their formal casting skills are either on hold or are slowly developing. Troll-walking is done on still water, line dumping is done on moving water, and dapping is done on both.

TROLL-WALKING

This does not refer to taking those little dolls with funny grins and fluorescent hair out for a walk. I first learned of this technique from Sam Slaymaker's book *Simplified Fly-Fishing* (Stackpole Books, Mechanicsburg, PA, 1988). The child stands at the shore of a pond (fig 4.1). She has pulled a quantity of line off the reel and through the tiptop. Now she tosses the pile of line onto the water. Pointing the rod tip toward the center of the pond, she walks its circumference. The line straightens out and trolls behind her. Ultimately the line drifts back to the shore, at which time she picks it up and the process is repeated.

This method is an outstanding way to take panfish provided that attention is paid to three details: select a body of water with relatively unobstructed shores (farm ponds are best); have your child step lightly so

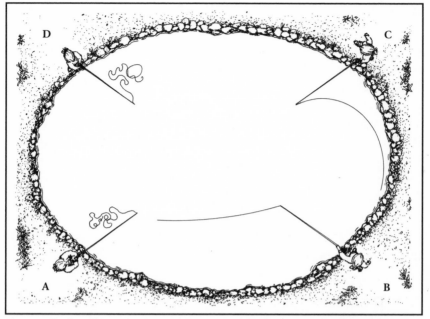

Fig. 4.1. Troll walking. a) A generous amount of fly line is tossed onto the water, and the rod tip is pointed toward the center of the pond. b) The line unfolds as the angler walks along the shore. c) Gradually the line drifts back to the shore. d) The line is gathered and tossed out, and the process is repeated.

that she does not spook the fish; and bring her to the pond when the fish are feeding in the shallows. During the summer months this means the early morning and evening hours and during the early spring and fall, the midafternoon.

LINE DUMPING

This is similar to troll-walking, except that your child stands still and flowing water imparts movement to the fly. Have your son walk upstream of a likely fish-holding spot and face downstream. He points his rod in a similar direction and tosses a pile of line on the water. Attached to the leader is a small streamer or a wet fly, say the Tupps Indispensable. Once the current straightens out the line, he begins the retrieve. Given that the fish may strike at any time the fly is on the water, including when there is a lot of slack on the surface, he must learn to set the hook not only by lifting the rod tip but also by simultaneously pulling in the slack with his line hand.

DAPPING

Your daughter will be communing with Dame Julianna herself when she employs this ancient and hallowed method of fly-fishing. She plays out enough line and leader so that the fly will just touch the surface when the rod is extended over the water (yet another reason to avoid buying short rods for children). By lifting the rod tip up and down she can make her artificial fly imitate a hovering insect. When she gently lowers the fly onto the surface film, a slashing strike will hopefully ensue. Chances are good if, instead of fishing blindly, your children take the time to spot fish and then dap them directly. Dapping is especially good on windy days that would foul your child's attempt at casting. The wind will add buoyancy to the leader and fly and thus enhance the impression of a fluttering insect. The standard dry flies such as the Adams or the Light Cahill are great for this type of fishing.

CASTING PRACTICE

Have you ever thought about visiting people in a foreign country? If you're able to speak their language fluently, you can become totally miscible in their society. Friends who have done this tell me that it's an enthralling experience. On the other hand, if you can't speak a word, you're lost. In between these two extremes is the comfortable state where you may not know all the semantic nuances, but you've learned enough of the language's key phrases to function reasonably well.

So it is when children journey to the land of fly-fishing and attempt to master its native language, casting. It would be wonderful if they were perfectly fluent, knew all the possible casts, and when to use them. This is hardly reasonable, at least for starters. One has only to read Joan Wulff's *Fly-Casting Techniques* (Lyons and Burford, New York, 1987), Mel Kreiger's *The Essence of Fly Casting* (Club Pacific, San Francisco, 1988), or Ed Jaworowski's *The Cast* (Stackpole Books, Mechanicsburg, PA, 1992) to realize that the number of possible casts available to the angler is rivalled only by the number of possible knots.

Without offending the masters, let me propose that your children need to learn only two casts—the roll cast and the traditional back and forward cast. Add to this a little line mending, and they will have acquired the key phrases of the foreign traveller, and they will be able to communicate—with fish! I don't want to sound anti-intellectual about this. If they're motivated, the parachute cast and the double haul will all come in time—presumably a much later time—but for now we want to get our little fly-fishing commandos on the water!

I'm not going to belabor the big-three skills. They are briefly outlined in appendix C. As instructor, you either know them already, or you can pick up any of a variety of books and videos and learn about them in exquisite detail. My two favorite sources for this information are the aforementioned book by Ed Jaworowski, and the video *Fly Casting With Lefty Kreh* (Tomorrow River Press, Gary Borger Enterprises, Inc., P.O.B. 1745, Wausau, WI 54402). I do need to make just one major comment about each of the skills:

First, don't begin with the back and forward cast; it's too difficult. Start with the roll cast. After dapping, dumping, and troll-walking, it's the simplest skill to master. This means that you will have to start near water. If you ignore this and try to roll cast on the lawn, your neighbors will be extremely amused (I know this from personal experience). The particular body of water you choose need not have fish in it. We use a man-made pond in a nearby office park.

Second, when it comes time for the back and forward cast, don't have your child hold the rod in the traditional near vertical position (fig. 4.2a). This juxtaposes his head between his casting hand and the travelling fly. Opt for the sidearm (fig. 4.2b) or the half-sidearm (fig. 4.2c) position. Not only will his head be out of the casting plane, but with the line closer to the surface of the water, he will be in excellent position to cast his fly under low-lying branches when the situation demands, and there will be less need to adjust for the effects of wind.

Speaking of wind, choose an absolutely still day to get your kids started on fly-casting. One of those doldrum days of August is just fine. Your experience will be less frustrating and a whole lot safer. How to defeat the wind is beyond the scope of this volume, but the references I cited earlier will put you on the right track.

An open lawn is a fine place to practice the back and forward cast. Make sure there is a leader on the line, and tie on a dummy fly. A piece of fluorescent yarn works fine. Bring along various lengths of rope, and lay out the lengths in circles on the grass, starting with relatively large circles close to the child. As she becomes more proficient, the circles can be made smaller and placed farther away. Offering small prizes tends to keep things exciting. I give my children nature stickers procured at a local

Fig. 4.2. The vertical arm position (left) is not recommended for children's casting. The sidearm (upper right) and half-sidearm (lower right) positions are preferable because the child's head is not juxtaposed between the casting hand and the rod tip.

Audubon store. It's important that every child get a reward. No matter how awkward the cast, there is almost always something about it that deserves praise, such as "Your feet were in exactly the right position" or "Good job for watching your backcast!" Be sure that even when they are casting the dummy flies, everyone is wearing hats and protective eyewear.

Third, most casting instructors justifiably praise the benefits of upstream mending. But don't forget to tell the kids that there is also a role for downstream mending. Having them mend upstream when the water under their line is flowing slower than the water under their fly is a major no-no.

の

When the weather is inclement or scheduling does not permit a trip to some open space, don't overlook indoor practice with the Fly-O. This device consists of a length of brightly colored yarn attached to a short rod and is available from Royal Wulff Products (HCR Box 70, Lew Beach, New York 12753). The great temptation that children face is to pretend that the Fly-Os are swords. It's a good idea to anticipate this travesty and warn them against any reenactment of the Crusades in your living room.

Kids will find Fly-O practice especially pleasant if they do it to music, particularly songs with heavy percussion. This would include disco music and even rap, provided that you can find a number with clean lyrics. If you're fortunate enough to have access to a video camera, film the children at work, and let them review and compare their performance with any of the commercially available videos on fly-casting. With relatively little input from you, they will be able to discover and correct their deficiencies, and you won't worry as much about their inadvertently picking up your own casting errors.

PLAYING AND LANDING PRACTICE

In truth, there is no way to faithfully replicate the playing and landing of a fish. The subtle communication that transpires between hunter and quarry via the gossamerlike leader is so complex that attempting to frame it within a series of exercises or even words seems to demean these revered acts. For practicing purposes, the best that a parent can do is offer the child a crude simulation. But even this is better than nothing, for it will permit her to discover the limits of her tackle, and also introduce her to the concept of line control. This is how it's done.

To mimic the setting of the hook, fully rig up her tackle minus the fly. Attach the tip of the leader to a large, heavy object, such as a table or chair. Strip out enough line so that when she faces the object with her rod held below horizontal, she will be about 20 feet away with no slack beyond the tiptop. Now have her *very gently* raise the rod tip to watch and feel how the rod loads. She can gradually increase the force and speed of this maneuver, but not by too much—you don't want her to rip off the tiptop. Besides, her initial quarry will not require the type of zealous hook setting used for tarpon or billfish.

Next have her add some slack to the line. When she practices setting the hook, she must now strip in line with her line hand to remove the slack while she lifts the rod tip. As before, have her start slowly and gently at first to protect the rod and better understand its dynamics.

Now tie the leader to a half-pound weight. After she performs the hook-setting motion, have her strip in line to "land" the weight without allowing any slack to develop in the line or permitting the line-leader connection to enter the tiptop.

The final step is to attach the leader to a live fish—and the fish is you! Hold the bare end of the leader and give a short tug to both signify the strike and signal her to perform the hook-setting motion. Once her rod is loaded, have her strip in line as you slowly walk toward her. Her job is to keep constant pressure on you without overloading the rod or allowing slack to develop in the line. Now is the time for you to really act like a fish. Periodically run away from her, at which time she lowers her rod to "bow to the fish," or run toward her to signal her need to strip in the resultant slack and keep the rod tip high. Stay vigilant; you don't want to run smack into her rod tip. This type of practice is great fun, good exercise for the fish and, provided you've got access to a large room, custom-made for rainy days. I do not however advise this activity without adult supervision, or you'll be sending your rod out for repairs.

WADING PRACTICE

This will look so weird, it will erase any of your neighbors' doubts that you are committable. On the other hand, it will ensure you that your kids will have been exposed to the principles of wading even before they set foot in the stream. It goes like this.

First, review with your kids the commandments of safe wading (see table 5.2). Next, select a strip of dry land to represent a stream. An inactive driveway will do nicely. Take several large objects, such as lawn chairs and bicycles, and place them in your stream to represent boulders. Use chalk to sketch some holes and drop-offs on the pavement. Also draw several arrows to indicate the direction of main current flow. Finally, place a wading staff and life vest at the side of your stream without attempting to call particular attention to them.

The game begins with your child standing on the bank. Tell him to wade across the stream. As he starts out he has a score of ten. For each error he makes en route, a point is subtracted from the total (table 4.1). When he is about half way across, be sure to tell him to stop, turn around to face you, and then turn again to continue on his way. Before reaching the opposite bank, he is told to pretend to fall into the water.

Be sure to score silently, particularly if your child is competing against other children. Otherwise your comments will give subsequent contestants an unfair advantage.

ɔ

TABLE 4.1

THE WADING GAME

Each child begins the game with a score of 10. For each of the following, a point is deducted from the total if the child:

1. Fails to don the life vest
2. Does not carry the wading staff
3. Moves straight across rather than diagonally to the path of the current
4. Lifts feet high off the streambed rather than correctly shuffling
5. Fails to keep the lead foot on the upstream side and pointed forward and the rear or anchor foot pointed downstream and at right angles to the lead foot
6. Rotates in a downstream rather than the correct upstream direction when executing all turns
7. Fails to probe for drop-offs and holes with wading staff
8. Crosses the upstream rather than the proper downstream side of holes
9. Does not take advantage of the slack water behind boulders to conserve energy while crossing
10. Does not place feet in a downstream direction after falling in

THE GREAT BUG CENSUS

The biggest difficulty with this game is that you go to the stream without your fly rod. You might feel embarrassed if your buddies see you nosing around for insects while they're hauling in the lunkers. Just dismiss this uncomfortable notion by remembering that Art Flick laid down his fly rod for three fishing seasons to study the sequential hatches on the Schoharie Creek in New York—and this effort made him immortal! Although you may not end up writing another *Streamside Guide*, you may immortalize yourself in your children's eyes by playing this fascinating game with them.

According to the rules, the stream is the nation, the bugs are its citizens, and your kids are the census takers. By turning over a few rocks, each child takes a turn sampling the stream. There is one point for each insect correctly identified (chapter 6), and a bonus point if the child can correctly identify whether the insect requires clean water, fairly clean water, or is pollution tolerant (chapter 10). High score wins, and each player may be allowed to recoup points by identifying organisms missed by the others. All insects are returned to the stream unharmed, otherwise there is automatic forfeiture. Also, be sure all of the rocks are carefully replaced to prevent any damage to the streambed.

THE REAL THING

Let's see now. Where do we stand? You've brought your kids to a trout stream. They've seen fly-fishers in action and decide they want a part of it. You've outfitted them along the lines of chapter 2, taught them how to line dump, dap, and troll-walk, and given them ample time to practice roll casting, line mending, and the traditional back and forward cast. They're well grounded in the rules of wading safely, and they've even picked up a little stream entomology. The only thing left is to fly-fish in the classic manner.

When starting off, I did not have my kids cast dry flies up and across or dead-drift nymphs. The amount of Zenlike concentration needed for these presentations would drive them from the stream and me crazy. Wet flies and streamers cast down and across are the way to go. Consider the advantages:

1. They are fishing a tight line, so the fish tend to hook themselves.
2. Drag is generally not a problem.
3. Downstream wading is less tiring than going upstream.
4. They will cover more water quickly.
5. You can let them do whatever they want after the cast is made. Regardless of whether they choose to impart action to the fly, nearly all strikes will occur at the end of the drift as the fly rises toward the surface.
6. They don't have to make this happen; the tightening of the line by the current does it for them.

When you do move on to dry flies, start with the bushy ones like Bivisibles and the Wulff series. These are sturdy, float well, and are easy to see. If the children still have trouble detecting strikes, don't hesitate in the slightest to commit heresy: put strike indicators on their leaders. Frederic Halford, the Father of Dry-Fly Angling, may turn over in his grave, but your kids will be into fish!

DEEPER WATERS

There is a common misunderstanding that fly-fishing must be relegated to the shallows. This is not entirely true, but the deeper your child wants to place her fly, the more weight she will have to add to her terminal tackle if she is sticking with a floating line. This means that both casting and strike detection become more difficult. And on those warm summer afternoons when the fish go deep, you may want to row out to the middle of the pond and try your luck anyway. Here are two techniques that may make these times more productive.

TROLLING
Since casting can be eliminated with this method, you can add all the split shot you want. Flies with keel hooks or weed guards will be helpful to avoid snagging the bottom. Strike detection may still be a problem.

THE SLIDING BOBBER
This technique can be used with either fly or spin-casting tackle and greatly enhances strike detection. I learned the fly-tackle version from articles by Dave Whitlock ("Panfish, Parts I and II," *Fly Fisherman*, May and July, 1991) and the spin-casting version from a nifty handbook supplied by E.J. "Dutch" Schaefers of Terminal Tactics, Inc. Dutch includes the handbook when you order those Custom Caddies I spoke about in chapter 2.

For the fly outfit (fig. 4.3) drill a hole longitudinally through an oval piece of balsa. Cut a short length of plastic tube from the handle portion of a cotton applicator, and glue it into the hole. Slide the bobber onto the leader. A thick knot should be in the leader just above the bobber. The distance from this knot to the fly should equal the distance you want the fly to sink. Now tie a weighted fly to the tippet end of the leader. When your child casts the fly, the bobber will abut the fly. After the fly hits the water and starts sinking, the leader will slip through the bobber until the bobber hits the stop knot.

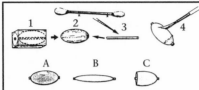

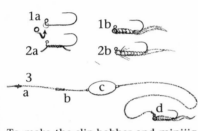

1. Mark a pattern for the bobber on a piece of balsa wood. 2. Cut and sand the wood to shape. 3. Insert and glue a section of hollow plastic or metal tube. 4. Paint the bobber a highly visible color. You can make the bobber with a regular shape (A), a quill shape (B) to reduce surface disturbance, or a popper shape (C).

To make the slip-bobber and minijig combo, weight a minijig as shown in 1a or 2a, tie it as you prefer (1b, 2b), and attach the bobber (3c) to the tippet as shown. Use a blood knot at 3a, a nail knot at 3b, and a clinch knot or improved clinch knot at 3d.

The slip-bobber and minijig combination allows the jig to sink to the proper depth and hold in a horizontal position. The bobber stays against the jig when it is cast.

Fig. 4.3. *The sliding bobber technique for the fly-rod outfit: assembly of the bobber (top left); the sliding bobber and minijig combination (lower left); and the rig in action (right)*

For spincasting gear, slide the A-JUST-A-BUBBLE (chapter 2) onto the line in the conventional manner with the wider end facing the fly. Do not twist the rubber core of the bubble so that it remains free to slide up and down the line. Also, do not open the plug to admit any water into the housing of the bubble. Place a piece of split shot on the line about four feet from the fly but below the bubble. Now decide how deep you want to fish. If it's nine feet, attach a piece of rubber band to the line using the method in fig. 4.4. Notice that the rubber band is located above the bobber and nine feet from the split shot. The band will be small enough to slide through the guides but large enough to stop the bubble from sliding on the line. Fish as you would the sliding balsa bobber on fly tackle. Reel in line gradually. When you find the feeding level of the fish, you can adjust the position of the rubber band (in the case of spin-casting gear) or the stop knot (with the fly-fishing outfit) so that each subsequent cast will put you in the honey spot.

THE OFF SEASON: AWAY FROM HOME

With fly-fishing only, catch-and-release stretches are becoming increasingly common on American streams, the concept of an "off season" is experiencing a slow but steady demise, since many of these areas can be legally fished throughout the year. For parents, this means that whether or not the kids go fishing is determined more by temperature than by month. According to my friend Paul Brodeur, who has been assiduously fishing the Farmington River for over 20 years, some of the best hatches and largest catches occur during those isolated and unexpectedly warm days in January and February, generally the harshest months of our New England winters.

Such lovely and rejuvenating respites are contrasted by the darker days when fly-fishing families must seek solace in other activities. Fortunately there are enough of them that your children's piscatorial pursuits need not lie dormant. Let's look at some of them now.

FISHING SHOWS

Kids love 'em, especially when it comes to popping in and out of the boats and campers that are on display, volunteering for the ubiquitous casting

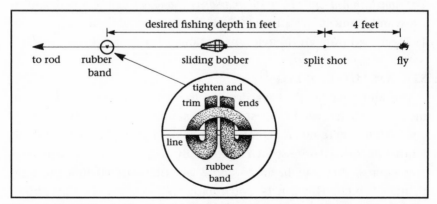

Fig. 4.4. The sliding-bobber technique for spin-casting outfits using the casting bubble.

instructors, and playing the mechanical fish on heavy saltwater gear. Our luck at trying for the live trout in the swimming pool, on the other hand, has been uniformly disappointing. I suspect those fish are so well fed they wouldn't dare look a worm in the eye, much less eat one.

SWIMMING LESSONS

This is something every angler should know (see chapter 5). Sign the kids up for winter classes at the Y. If they already swim well, sign them up for advanced classes so that they will swim even better.

VISIT A FISH HATCHERY

The big ones have indoor aquaria and walk-through exhibits. Schedule your visit around feeding time so the kids can learn about hierarchies within fish populations. If you are going with a group, see if a hatchery employee will be available to lead a discussion or answer questions.

FIRST AID

If you want your children to be true outdoorsmen, they will need to know this topic thoroughly. Who knows, yours may be the life they save! The American Red Cross offers a first-aid course specifically designed for kids of ages 8–10 years. It's called Basic Aid Training. For a modest fee they will receive a total of eight hours of instruction that covers such topics as minor and severe bleeding, burns, how to respond to breathing emergencies, and how to identify and prevent potentially harmful situations. Standard first-aid courses are offered for older children and adults. If such courses are not available in your area, give some deep thought to buying *The American Red Cross First Aid and Safety Handbook* by the American Red Cross and Kathleen A. Handal, M.D., Little, Brown and Company, Boston, 1992, and go through the relevant sections with your kids.

STREAM MONITORING

If you and your family have decided to adopt a stream (chapter 10), monitoring activities do not stop when summer vacation comes to an end. While you're out together, why not have the kids create a photo journal of their favorite stretch of river? By comparing winter and summer photos, they can begin to appreciate the seasonal influences on riparian habitat. This can be particularly well demonstrated by photographing sequential sections of streambank at each of the four seasons, and then taping the photos next to each other in close register. Encourage them to share their photos and stream monitoring activities with their class or scout troop.

THE OFF SEASON: AT HOME

Think of these as indoor outings. Here are our family's favorites.

FLY-TYING

If you doubt that your kids can handle this, turn to chapter 8. Not only is fly-tying the very best way to keep the sport alive in the dead of winter, it can be a source of tremendous self-esteem for your children. Last winter my kids and I volunteered to help staff the Connecticut Fly Fishermen's booth at the annual fishing show in Hartford. As part of that endeavor, club members set up their vises and tie for the onlookers. Not far into the afternoon, we made an interesting observation. When the adults were tying, kids drifted by with hardly a glance. When my children were tying, hoards of kids huddled around the table. The reason was obvious: Seeing their peers tie told the kids that this was something they could do; gray hair and a widening midriff were not prerequisites.

That was the first of their public demonstrations. They have since tied for the scouts, as well as for disabled children at Newington Children's Hospital. When their grammar school hosted Hobby Day, they were the only kids who showed up with tying vises and feathers. Seeing the pride on their faces when their classmates took so much interest in their creations told me that our family was onto something special.

There is yet another advantage to fly-tying: its use as a social solvent. As I write, it's a cold November day. The family is feeling a bit of cabin fever. Last night Amy and I had a disagreement. We arrived at an uneasy truce, and she went into her room to read Nancy Drew, while I went to my study to tie some flies. I was half into a Gold-Ribbed Hare's Ear when she entered the room and sheepishly asked, "Can I tie too?" Now my desk consists of a very long door on top of two filing cabinets; I wanted a large desk top so that we would always have room to tie side by side. She smiled as I nodded and set up her vise. For several minutes we tied in silence. Then she got to a difficult part in her creation, an intriguing combination of crystal chenille, purple marabou, and fluorescent pink hackle. "Dad, can you help me out?" she asked. I looked at her with all my love and admiration. The ice had melted between us, and we were back on track again.

Fly-tying is also an excellent way of addressing The Wall. If you are a parent, I'm sure you know what The Wall is all about. The kids come home from school. You give them a big hug and say, "Well, how did things go today?" Instantly all expression leaves their faces and they become electively mute. If you press on with your inquiry you can possibly induce them to eke out a paltry "Uh, OK I guess." Any further prodding is useless, and you realize that once again you have encountered The Wall and it is insurmountable—or so I thought.

Once it was clear to us that fly-tying was not going to be just a passing fancy, we decided that we would have to make some special time for it to avoid conflicts with our mutually busy schedules. So, two or three nights a week, sandwiched between bathtime and their prayers, we tie a few flies together. The kids are really relaxed after their baths, they're comfortably nestled in their pajamas, and the only concession to formality is that they have to slip on a pair of shoes in case any errant hooks find their way to the floor. Not long after these sessions started, I came upon a remarkable discovery. Once their fingers were occupied with feathers, tinsel, and chenille, they started talking about all of their trials, tribulations, and victories of the day. It was as if the mere physical act of fly-tying had released them from the shackles of reticence. In some obscure manner, this shared activity provided a sense of security and openness that could not be reached by mere parental interrogation. I continue to be amazed each time this happens.

READING ALOUD

This should not cease when your kids learn to read independently. People of all ages like to be read to. It's cozy, and gives your imagination a workout. Where to start? Do *not* reach for *The Compleat Angler* unless your object is to propel them into a state of profound stupor. Try instead *The Fishing River* by Edythe Records Warner (The Viking Press, New York, 1962). Although this book is now sadly out of print, many public libraries still fortunately hold copies. It is a boy's gently rolling memoir of his days spent fly-fishing with his brother and grandfather on the Kinnikinick River in Wisconsin. Although certainly not a "how-to" book, just about every major aspect of trout fishing, from fly selection to stream restoration, is touched upon in this slender volume. I first read this story to

Christopher as we were huddled on the couch on two chilly winter evenings. I know it was a success because he asks that I read it to him again and again.

An absolute must is *The River God* by the British playwright Roland Pertwee. If you appreciate a challenge, try reading this story aloud to your children without having your voice periodically buckle with emotion. *The River God* made its first appearance in a 1928 issue of *The Saturday Evening Post* and has been subsequently reprinted in several anthologies, including *River Gods and Spotted Devils* (edited by John Culler and Chuck Wechsler, LiveOak Press, Camden, South Carolina, 1988) and *The One That Got Away: A Treasury of Fishing Stories* (edited by Martin Greenberg and Charles Waugh, Crown Publishers, Inc., New York, 1989).

I first learned of this literary gem from Phil Genova, a member of the Federation of Fly Fishers whose intense interest in teaching children the craft has culminated in his creation of the Fly Fisher Apprentice Program. At a recent meeting of the Northeast Council of the F.F.F., both of my children benefitted greatly from the instruction offered by Phil's enthusiastic team. The day's activities were organized so that children had the opportunity to teach children. The apprentice program also makes available a variety of printed instructional materials. For more information, you can write to Phil at 407 West Seneca St., Ithaca, New York 14850.

KNOT TYING PRACTICE
This activity will appeal to children's competitive spirit if it is presented as a game. Author and fly-fisherman Bill Tapply suggests timing their knot tying with a stopwatch, or challenging them to tie the knots behind their backs or with their eyes closed. As with the aforementioned casting practice, I recommend that every child wins for something, such as hardest knot to untie.

VIDEOS
One does not have to be a member of the Rand Corporation to realize that kids and television are pretty much inseparable. Unfortunately, there is no end to the drivel that's on the tube, and although some gems do exist, let's face it: Between Sesame Street for the little tykes and Masterpiece Theatre for us old geezers, there is an expanse of intellectual tundra that wouldn't edify an amoeba much less a growing child. You may wish to at least partially fill the void with fly-fishing videos, but here you must step

carefully, as if you were negotiating the slippery rocks of Hendrickson's Pool on the Beaverkill.

Many fly-fishing videos are manna for adults but are highly unlikely to stimulate the sporting appetite of a child. You know the ones I mean, where casting gurus demonstrate the technowizardry involved in executing the air-mended reverse tuck cast, or the ones that plunge you into the subspecies identification of certain nearly extinct caddisflies. There are others however that are as delightful for children as adults. This was brought home to me in a very compelling way.

Chris was six years old and we were spin-casting for bluegill on a Catskill lake. In short order he was fast to his first fish ever and soon landed the four-inch monster. When I offered to unhook the fish, he said, "Let me do it, Dad." He gently removed the barbless hook, cradled the fish beneath its belly, and rocked it back and forth beneath the surface of the water. As the fish slipped away from his fingers he looked up at me and said, "Catch-and-release." I was thunderstruck because *I had not yet breathed a word about C&R to him.* After a moment I regained my composure and managed to ask him where he had picked up this information. He told me that Dave Whitlock had taught it to him. I was pondering how Dave had managed to move into our neighborhood and meet my son without my knowing about it when I remembered that we owned several of his videotapes. I had viewed these many times, often with Chris sitting silently beside me on the couch. Hence we both had numerous opportunities to watch Dave demonstrate the proper methods of C&R, and I had obviously not been the only one paying attention!

I was dizzy with pride. Here I was with my little angling buddy on our very first fishing trip together. Although I had every intention of eventually introducing him to C&R, he had already embraced the ethic. I gave him a big hug and, later that night, after he had released many more bluegill and one truly formidable pickerel, we repaired to the Antrim Lodge where I treated him to a Cranberry Smash, a refreshing concoction of cranberry juice and orange sherbet, and revelled in the power of video.

Besides Dave's videos there are several others that your kids will find memorable. I don't know of any youngster who has seen Trout Unlimited's *Way of the Trout* and not been swept away by it. For older children and adolescents, Gary Borger's *Where the Trout Are* stands as a monument to sound environmental thought. The man has made many excellent contributions, but with this work he deserves to be beatified. All children

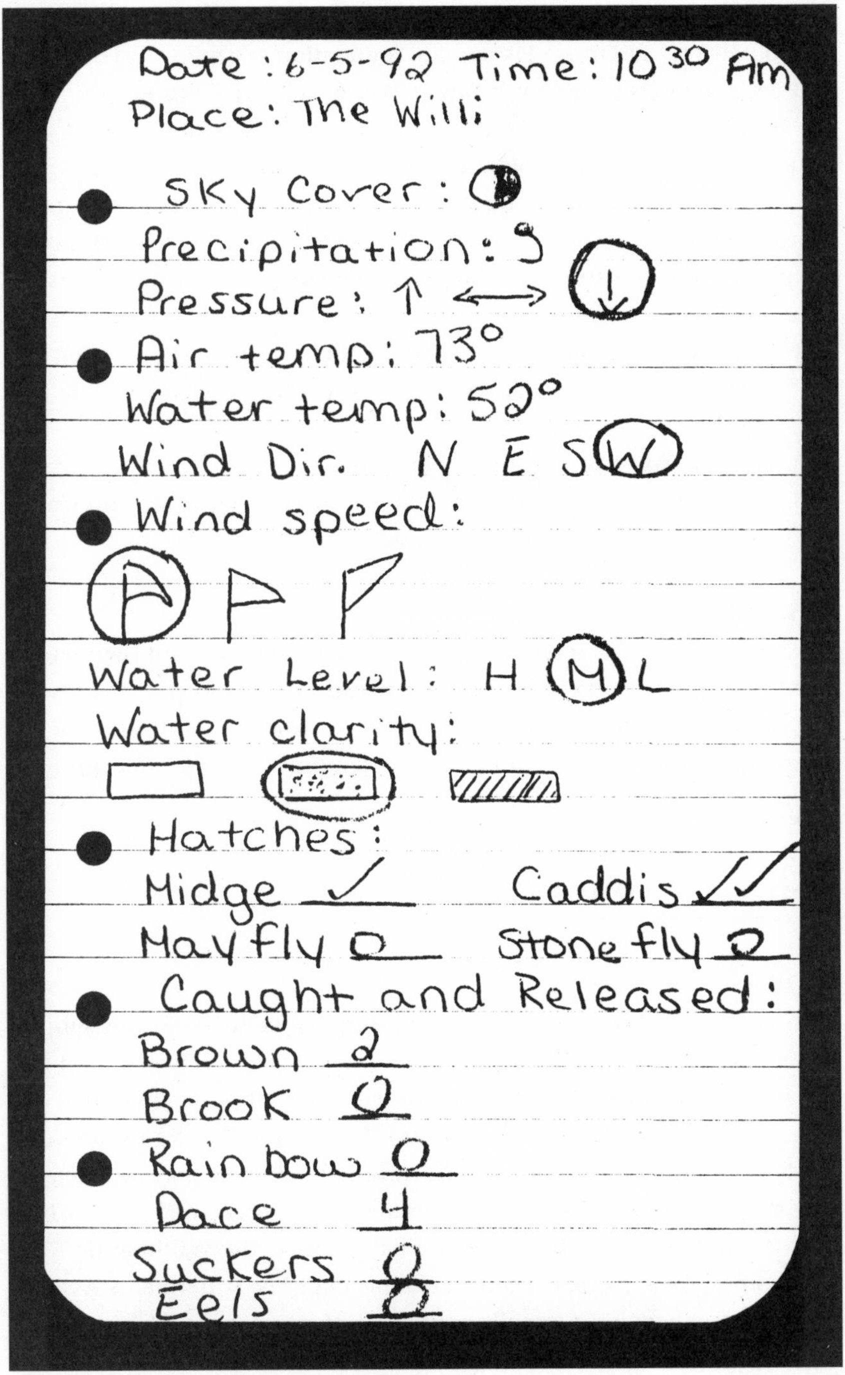

Date: 6-5-92 Time: 10³⁰ Am
Place: The Willi

- Sky Cover: ◑
- Precipitation: ⌇
- Pressure: ↑ ←→ ⊘↓
- Air temp: 73°
- Water temp: 52°
- Wind Dir. N E S Ⓦ
- Wind speed:

  Ⓐ ⌐ ⌐

  Water Level: H Ⓜ L
  Water clarity:

  ▭ ⬭ ▨

- Hatches:
  Midge ✓   Caddis ✓✓
  Mayfly 0   Stonefly 2
- Caught and Released:
  Brown 2
  Brook 0
- Rainbow 0
  Dace 4
  Suckers 0
  Eels 0

Fig. 4.5. A page from Amy's field journal

should see the video shorts *Hooked on Fishing—Not on Drugs* and *Pass it On* distributed by the Future Fisherman Foundation (chapter 7). For young fly-tiers, the Orvis Company's *Save A Worm—Tie A Fly* has no peer. This can be followed with Eric Pettine's *How to Tie Flies* (Warburton Productions, Inc., Fort Collins, Colorado 80526).

One issue that may come up about acquiring videos is cost. Although many are reasonably priced, some of the more limited-production items put more of a strain on the purse. When choosing videos, consider the following:

1. Kids, unlike adults, love watching their favorite shows over and over. If it's a video that you know they'll like, the cost will be well worth it.
2. Fess up. You like watching them too.
3. Your kids can always show the tape to their scout troop and loan it to their teachers to show in class.

DESIGN A FIELD JOURNAL

Buy your child an inexpensive spiral-bound pocket pad, and then let her decide how she wants to record her streamside observations. Kids are especially intrigued by codes and ciphers, so I taught Amy some of the standard weather symbols that she has chosen to incorporate into her journal (fig. 4–5).

SOME FINAL COMMENTS

FOOD

In discussing outings with children it is impossible to avoid this subject. It is especially germane here because the relationship between food and the angler is complex. I've silently studied this matter for some time and have reached some startling conclusions. Foremost is that fly-fishers don't eat. Sounds impossible, but it's true. Although my little gray cells tell me that they must eat sometime, it's certainly not when they're anywhere near the water. I recall some intense days fishing the Willimantic River with some fellow members of the Connecticut Fly Fishermen's Association. Guys who would normally scarf down three pepperoni pizzas apiece for lunch would go all day without a morsel, so intent were they upon their quarry. At the very best, by late afternoon someone might extract a

∾

FAST FUN FOOD FOR FLY-FISHING FORAYS

1. Fresh, washed, uncooked peas in pods
2. Carrot slices dipped in peanut butter
3. Fresh, washed, uncooked green beans
4. Celery stalks filled with a mixture of grated cheese, minced red pepper, and mayonnaise
5. Sandwiches of fresh tomato, cucumber, and sweet onion with butter
6. Cream cheese and raisins spread on rice cakes
7. Nuts mixed in plain yoghurt and sweetened with honey
8. Green pepper halves stuffed with cottage cheese
9. Trail mix (raisins, nuts, sunflower seeds, and carob chips)
10. One-to-one mixture of pineapple and cranberry juice for warm mornings; hot chocolate from the thermos on cold mornings

miniature candy bar from his vest and then divide it piecemeal among five or six companions. Most would refuse the offering. This drove me to either of two possible explanations: Fly-fishers own gastrointestinal tracts that are anatomically and physiologically distinct from the rest of the population, or their hypothalami, the eating centers of their brains, march to the time of a far different biological clock.

Kids do not figure comfortably into this scenario. They love food, especially junk food. To plan an outing without some recognition of their alimentary needs is sheer folly. Regardless of whether there are monster browns rising everywhere, the first question my kids ask me when we arrive on the water is, "What's there to eat?" It's fun to pack a surprise for them, but it needn't be all potato chips and chocolate. Some healthy alternatives that require minimal preparation and no cooking are listed in table 4.2. For additional ideas consult Jan Brink and Melinda Ramm's *Snacks: Speedy, Nutritious and Cheap Kid's Snacks* (New American Library, New York, 1984). Streamside dining can be quite delightful; we've had some of our best conversations on these occasions. After the meal the kids should understand that no fly touches the water until all the refuse is picked up and disposed of properly.

WHEN TO STOP

Someone once asked Picasso, "What is the secret of your genius?" He answered that a good artist knows not only when to draw, but when to stop. The same can be said of fly-fishing. Children's attention span for the sport is likely to fluctuate on a day-to-day or even an hour-to-hour basis. Parents who have developed a constant and long-abiding devotion to the sport are likely to find this vacillation frustrating. Trying to overcome it by insisting that the children fish is doomed to failure. You cannot force-feed them fly-fishing any more than you can force-feed them their vegetables. The best you can do is make the sport look, like the vegetables, as attractive as possible and hope that they will develop an appetite for it. And if an outing starts to turn poorly because the child's interest lies elsewhere on that particular day, take a tip from Picasso: know that it's time to stop.

CHAPTER FIVE

SAFETY

Thus far we have touched on a number of safety issues, from protective eyewear and hats to long rods, barbless hooks, and preferred casting positions. In this chapter we will expand on these issues considerably. Advanced safety planning will at least save you and your family some inconvenience when you are on the water. At most it will help you avoid hardship.

WADING

Wading will not only permit your children to reach more fish, they will find it fun in its own right. A fundamental rule of fly-fishing is that you should not wade if you can't swim, so swimming lessons are as important as your children's casting lessons. And if you wade but don't swim, now is the time to correct that discrepancy.

All children who wade should wear personal flotation devices (PFDs). The PFD should be complementary to, not a substitute for the child's swimming ability. I know this tarnishes the image of the traditionally attired angler, but the extra margin of safety is worth the lapse in sartorial taste.

Selecting the proper PFD involves some care. It should have a U.S. Coast Guard Approval Number, and be sure you select the right type (table 5.1). Generally the decision is a trade-off between bulk and protection. The safest PFDs tend to be the bulkiest and may be uncomfortable and cumbersome when casting.

Most families will find that a Type II or III PFD offers a reasonable compromise. It should fit your child well. If you pick up the child by the

TABLE 5.1

TYPES OF PERSONAL FLOTATION DEVICES*

TYPE	INDICATIONS	ADVANTAGES
I. Off-shore life jacket	Open, rough, or remote water where rescue may be slow coming	Floats you the best; turns most unconscious wearers face-up in the water; highly visible color
II. Near-shore buoyant vest	Calm, inland water or where there is good chance of fast rescue	Turns some unconscious wearers face-up in the water; less bulky; more comfortable than type I
III. Flotation aid	Same as II	Generally the most comfortable type for continuous wear; freedom of movement; many styles
IV. Throwable device	Calm inland water with heavy boat traffic, where help is always nearby	Can be thrown to someone; good backup to wearable PFDs; some can be used as seat cushion
V. Special-use devices	Limited to special uses or conditions	Made for specific activities
VI. Hybrid inflatable device**	Same as types I, II, or III as noted on the label; *not for kids*	Least bulky of all types; high flotation when inflated; good for continuous wear

* Data obtained from U.S. Coast Guard Academy, New London, Connecticut

** Hybrid PFDs contain some conventional flotation material and are also inflatable. *They are not approved for use by children.*

DISADVANTAGES	KINDS
Bulky	Two sizes to fit most children and adults
Not for long hours in rough water; will not turn some unconscious wears face-up in water	Infant, small child, medium child, adult
Not for rough water; wearer may have to tilt head back to avoid face-down position in water	Small child through adult
Not for unconscious persons; not for non-swimmers or children; not for many hours in rough water	Cushions, rings, horseshoe buoys
See label for limits of use	Boardsailing vests, deck suits, work vests, hybrid PFDs, etc.
May not adequately float some wearers unless partially inflated; requires active use and care of inflation chamber	Various

COURTESY STEARNS MANUFACTURING COMPANY

Fig. 5.1. The Stearns fishing vest for children (model #4120) is also a type III personal flotation device.

shoulders of the PFD, his chin and ears should not slip through. Don't get one that's too large under the pretense that he will grow into it. This is false economy because it's dangerous. He needs the protection now, as he's entering the water. If he grows out of it get him another one that fits. This is one area where you do not want to mess up.

Some PFDs are designed to double as fishing vests and come in children's sizes. The Stearns Manufacturing Company, P.O. Box 1498, St. Cloud, Minnesota, 56302 makes a Youth Fishing Vest (model # 4120) that meets U.S. Coast Guard Type III standards and will fit children from 50–

ɾʒ

TABLE 5.2

RULES FOR SAFE WADING

1. Never allow your kids to wade in water that you are not personally familiar with.
2. Kids should not wade unless they are receiving continuous eye-contact supervision from a qualified adult.
3. Always wear a U.S. Coast Guard-approved PFD.
4. Always carry a wading staff.
5. Wear footwear appropriate for the type of streambed on which you are wading.
6. If wearing chest-high waders, a snug wading belt should also be worn.
7. Stay away from riverbanks that are eroding and unstable.
8. Cross at an angle to, rather than directly across the path of the main current.
9. Probe the bottom with the wading staff before advancing.
10. Shuffle across the streambed rather than stepping highly.
11. The lead foot should be on the upstream side and pointed forward; the rear or anchor foot should be pointed downstream at right angles to the lead foot.
12. The anchor foot should not cross in front of the lead foot.
13. Cross on the downstream side of holes and drop-offs.
14. When turning around, rotate in an upstream direction.
15. Use the slack water behind boulders as a resting spot to conserve energy while crossing.
16. If you fall in, point your feet in a downstream direction and allow the current to bring you to a spot where you can safely exit the stream.
17. If you fall in, concentrate on saving yourself rather than your tackle.
18. Watch out for rising water levels below dams and during rising tides.

90 pounds with chest sizes 26–29 inches (fig. 5.1). (These vests are distributed in Canada by Ranpro, Inc., Victoria Street and Ireland Road, P.O. Box 430, Simcoe, Ontario N3Y 4L6, at (519) 426-1094.) Avoid vests that inflate either manually or by CO_2 cartridge. These are not recommended because children may not be able to quickly inflate the vest in an emergency situation.

Once your kids are equipped with the proper PFD, have them enter a supervised swimming pool while wearing it so they will learn what it feels like if they take an accidental dunking in the pond or stream. With a relaxed posture and the head tilted back, the PFD should keep your child's chin above water and he should be able to breathe easily.

A PFD, like the rest of your tackle, requires maintenance. Before putting it away, let it drip dry. Never use a direct heat source such as a radiator or heater to dry it. Check for punctures, rips, mildew, and waterlogging. If the PFD contains kapok, squeeze it. If there is an air leak, get rid of it. And don't forget to inscribe your child's name on the vest!

Two other items essential for safe wading are proper footwear and a wading staff. Rubber cleats are good for sandy or silt bottoms, while felt soles are designed for algae-covered rocks. For extremely slippery bottoms, metal cleats are recommended. I view stream bottoms that require metal cleats as too dangerous for my children, so this last point is a moot one for our family. If I am not sure about a particular streambed, I will ask the locals first *and* wade it myself before allowing my kids to enter the water.

I make liberal use of a wading staff and expect my children to do the same. Shallow water is no exception. In fact, falls in shallow water are more likely to result in bruises and fractures because the cushioning effect of the water is diminished. It is essential that the staff fit the child properly. Have her stand upright with her arm extended in front of her, slightly flexed at the elbow. This will enable you to determine her correct grip position (fig. 5.2). A mop handle made of ash that comes with one of those metal tips meant to screw into the mop head works fine. Trim off the excess handle above the grip position and whip some cord for a handle (fig. 5.3). Drill a hole through the staff below the grip position and thread a lanyard through the hole. A clasp is placed on the lanyard so she can attach the staff to her belt. Be sure the lanyard is not so long that she will trip over it. The staff can be finished with paste wax or a marine-quality spar varnish. If you're good at woodworking, carving in your child's name and some decorative flourishes will certainly be appreciated.

As I mentioned in chapter 2, my children wade in one fashion only: wet in warm weather wearing felt-soled high-topped sneakers. When the time comes to buy them waders, I will get them the chest-high type with a snug wading belt rather than hippers, since the latter are more likely to

Fig. 5.2. To determine the proper grip position on a wading staff, the child's arm should be extended forward with the elbow slightly flexed.

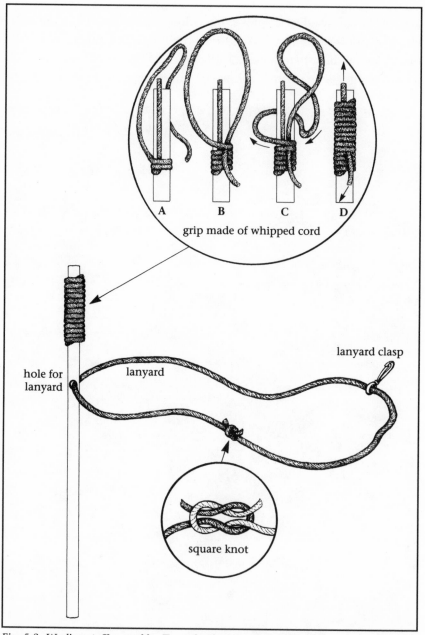

grip made of whipped cord

A B C D

lanyard clasp

hole for lanyard

lanyard

square knot

Fig. 5.3. Wading staff assembly. To make the grip: a) Lay the cord parallel to the end of the staff with one end protruding from it. Take the other end of the cord and make five or six turns around both the cord and the staff, working toward the end of the staff. b) Make a loop with the cord, laying it parallel to the staff in the reverse direction. c) Grab the loop and turn it around the staff and both ends of the cord at least six to eight times. d) Pull the loop through the whipping and trim off both loose ends of cord.

fill with water if they fall in. Waders that fit improperly are unsafe, and finding a brand that fits your child correctly may take some effort: men's small sizes and women's models may still be too large. Recently Neo-Sports Manufacturing Company, 1600 Sky Park Drive, Medford, Oregon 97504, has come out with a Trico Youth Neoprene Wader that is available in three different children's sizes.

One last point. The supervision you give your children when they wade should be no less than when they swim. This means that you must maintain continual eye contact with them. It is impossible to do this if you are fishing yourself. If you can't or are unwilling to provide this level of supervision, the kids should get out of the water.

Rules for safe wading were introduced in chapter 4 and are amplified in table 5.2. Keep them on hand and go over them with your children before each outing until it becomes second nature to them.

FIRST AID AND SOME COMMENTS ON HOOK REMOVAL

A small vest-pocket-sized first-aid kit has increased my sense of security when I'm on the water with Chris and Amy. On more than one occasion, the kit has obviated our need to leave the water and, in some cases, go hunting for a pharmacy. I often find myself dispensing first-aid materials to nearby anglers who are not so equipped. This has initiated and cemented a number of friendships.

In addition to the usual adhesive bandages, antiseptic ointment, gauze pads, and tweezers, the kit includes chewable acetaminophen (no need to find fresh water to swallow the tablets) and a loop of stiff monofilament to help in removing barbed hooks (fig. 5.4). This last item might seem incongruous, since we only use barbless hooks that in most cases can simply be removed by backing them out the way they went in. However, there is no guarantee that we will not be impaled by the barbed hook of another angler, so the loop can come in handy.

The first thing to do if your kids get stuck is to decide whether you should be the one removing the hook. If the hook has lodged in the delicate structures of the head or neck, in bone, the tendons of the hands or feet, or near an artery, go to your nearest hospital. When lodged in other areas, the loop removal method can be attempted (fig. 5.5). You can practice this by sticking a barbed hook into an orange. The orange provides a texture similar to human skin—medical and nursing students

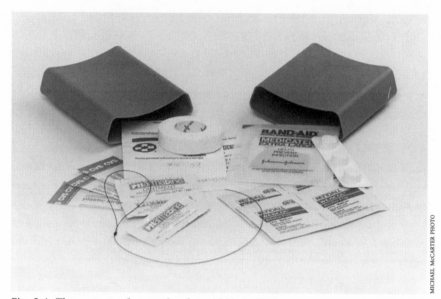

Fig. 5.4. The contents of my pocket first-aid kit include a loop of stiff monofilament for hook removal.

practice giving shots to oranges before going on to patients. The leader is cut off the hook, and a loop of stout monofilament is slid over the shank of the hook to the bend. Press the eye of the hook down to the surface of the orange with one hand. With the other, pull firmly on the loop to extract the hook. Dress the wound by applying an antibiotic solution and then a sterile gauze pad. Do not use an antibiotic ointment or tape the hole closed. These manueuvers can seal off the puncture wound and thus promote infection.

For barbed hooks that have penetrated the skin and then turned, the

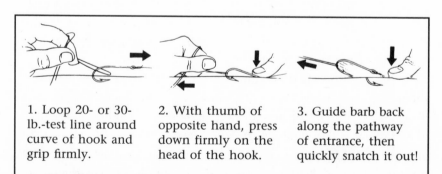

1. Loop 20- or 30-lb.-test line around curve of hook and grip firmly.

2. With thumb of opposite hand, press down firmly on the head of the hook.

3. Guide barb back along the pathway of entrance, then quickly snatch it out!

Fig. 5.5. The loop method of hook removal.

loop method does not work. There is a method of removal that involves pushing the point and barb up through the skin, cutting them off with a wire cutter, and then backing out the remainder of the hook. I do *not* recommend that you do this to children. In such cases, bring your child to the nearest emergency room where a doctor will inject local anesthetic and make the whole process a lot less painful for all of you.

Since hook jabs are the commonest type of fishing-related injuries, check that your children's tetanus immunizations are up to date before venturing astream.

In addition to the pocket first-aid kit, I keep a backup "master" kit in the car. The contents are listed in table 5.3. On the inside lid of the kit I've taped four additional items: change for a pay phone, a list of emergency phone numbers pertaining to our own locale, a blank card to enter emergency numbers for places we are visiting, and a checklist of the kit's contents. Once a month I go through the kit, consulting the checklist and replenishing any supplies as needed. If you do not have one of these kits already, consider having the children help you assemble one. It's a great

---

⋐⋑

TABLE 5.3

A MASTER FIRST-AID KIT

TOOLS: Bandage scissors, bulb syringe, candle, chemical cold packs, cotton balls, cotton swabs, cup, disposable gloves, eyecup, first-aid guide, flashlight, forceps, pencil and pad, safety pins, sling, soap, splint, thermometer, waterproof matches

FOR DRESSING WOUNDS: Adhesive strips, aquaphor dressing, bandage rolls, elastic bandage, iodine solution, sterile eye-gauze and nonstick pads, tincture of benzoin, waterproof hypoallergenic tape, wound-closure strips

MEDICATIONS: Activated charcoal, antiseptic ointment and wipes, calamine lotion, chewable acetaminophen, sterile eyewash, syrup of ipecac

KEPT NEXT TO KIT: Extra set of clothes for each member of the fishing party, space blankets, supply of fresh water

---

family project for a rainy day. But remember that owning all of these items is of little help if you do not know how and when to use them properly. For this information consult *The American Red Cross First Aid and Safety Handbook* by the American Red Cross and Kathleen A. Handal, M.D. (Little, Brown and Company, Boston, 1992), and sign them up for a first-aid course sponsored by your local Red Cross chapter.

Fig. 5.6. Defense against Ixodes dammini: *hat, light-colored clothing, long sleeves and pants, shirt tucked in, socks pulled up over cuffs, and closed shoes.*

LYME DISEASE

Fly-fishers love to wallow in Latin terminology and are known to mumble comments such as "The *Salmo trutta* are rising to *Paraleptophlebia adoptiva*" instead of just saying "The browns are munching blue quills." Two other Latin genera and species worth knowing about are *Borrelia burgdorferi* and *Ixodes dammini*. Unfortunately, these do not refer to graceful mayflies or acrobatic trout. The former is the major microorganism causing Lyme disease and the latter is the tick whose bite transmits it.

Fly-fishers have to be wary about Lyme disease not only because the tick thrives in riparian habitat, but also because it feeds most actively from May through October, prime fishing season. The bite is usually painless, but what comes after is not. Early symptoms may include a flulike illness, joint pain, and a skin rash. Later, heart and nervous system damage as well as a crippling arthritis may ensue.

The good news is that if treated early, Lyme disease is curable. The bad news is that many people do not know how to take steps to prevent the disease or to recognize it in its early stages. If you go fly-fishing with your kids, you especially need to know these things. Everyone should wear hats, light-colored clothing (to help spot the ticks), tucked-in shirts with long sleeves, socks pulled up over the cuffs of long pants, and closed shoes (fig. 5.6). Use commercial tick repellant on the clothing.

When you return home from a day's outing, immediately inspect all clothing and dump it into the washing machine. Then inspect each other's bodies carefully. In our home we call this the "tick check." This includes looking through hair as well as along hairlines, around the eyes, in the ears, and within the armpits and other body folds. Don't expect that showering will wash off the tick. The insect's mouthparts are lined with a series of barbs just like the ones on fish hooks and consequently its hold is tenacious.

The lyme tick is much smaller than the common American dog tick (fig. 5.7), so you've got to look carefully and in good light. Once the tick

Fig. 5.7. From left to right: actual size of larva, nymph, adult male, adult female, and engorged adult female Ixodes *ticks; and, by comparison, adult male and female common dog ticks.*

engorges itself with blood, it may become several times larger, yet still be only about the size of the head of a common pin. The tick transmits the disease while it is feeding, but not all ticks carry the germ and not all tick bites result in Lyme disease. I can't overemphasize the need for early inspection, because ticks usually crawl around for several hours before burying their feeding tube into the skin.

If you do find a tick, remove it by grasping its mouthparts where they enter the skin with a pair of fine-pointed tweezers; do *not* crush the tick's body. Tug firmly and repeatedly until the bug comes off. The important thing is to remain calm, especially in front of your kids.

Don't throw the tick away. Put it in a covered jar of alcohol. I keep such a jar in my vest. The jar has a blank label so that I can enter the date, body location of the bite, and the place where I think the bite occurred. This information and the specimen can help the doctor identify the tick. State and local boards of health also can assist in identification. This can be important since some species other than *Ixodes dammini* have been reported to transmit the disease.

Early symptoms of Lyme disease include a slowly expanding red rash. This is seen in about 80 percent of people treated for Lyme disease. The rash may appear days to weeks after the tick bite. Partial clearing may

---

∓

TABLE 5.4

SYMPTOMS AND SIGNS
OF EARLY LYME DISEASE

COMMON	LESS COMMON
Rash	Swollen Glands
Headache	Enlarged spleen
Fever chills	Chest, ear, or back pain
Fatigue	Dizziness
Nausea	Sun sensitivity
Flulike illness	Sore throat
Stiff neck	Dry Cough
Pains in muscles and joints	Testicular swelling
Joint swelling	

---

develop in the center of the rash, but actually the rash can take any of several forms, so it is best to have any new skin eruption checked by your doctor. Not recalling the tick bite should not prevent you from doing so: Many patients with Lyme disease don't recall the bite. Other symptoms to be concerned about are listed in table 5.4.

While you're at it, don't forget your bird dog. Pets also have to be examined. Ticks are removed the same way, and it pays to be aware of the various tick collars, sprays, and dips that are available for pets.

If you need more information about Lyme disease ask your doctor or call your state department of health, or your local chapter of the Arthritis Foundation (1-800-541-8350).

BEE STINGS

If the bee's stinger is lodged in the skin, remove it by scraping it off with a fingernail or card. Squeezing the stinger with forceps will only release more venom under the skin. Wash the site with soap and water and apply a cold pack to reduce pain and swelling and retard the spread of the venom. Watch for any severe allergic reaction. Children with known history of such reactions should wear a medical I.D. bracelet and carry their emergency allergy medication.

SNAKE BITES

Lucky for us that most snakes in North America are not venomous. The poisonous ones are the pit vipers (rattlesnakes, copperheads, and water moccasins) and coral snakes. Since the type of care you administer depends on the type of snake that did the biting, it's worthwhile becoming familiar with reptilian field marks. Field guides are helpful, but the best way to acquire this knowledge is to visit a zoo where the snakes can be viewed close up. If you or your children get bitten and you're not sure if the snake was poisonous, respond as if it was.

Venomous bites are no joke. Check the victim's airway, breathing, and circulation and, if needed, institute resuscitative measures. Send another angler to call for emergency medical help. The nearest hospital can be directed to start preparing the correct antivenom. The bite should be cleaned with soap and water and, since the affected part may swell, any constrictive clothing should be removed. The victim should lie still and the site of the bite should be comfortably immobilized and placed below the level of his heart. Shock can sometimes develop, so you should learn how to recognize and respond to this emergency. Things not to do include applying cold compresses to the bite, cutting into the bite, applying a tourniquet, raising the site of the injury above the level of the victim's heart, asking him to exercise, or administering any aspirin or pain medication without a physician's go-ahead. If you plan to fish in an area where poisonous snakes have been reported, carry a snake-bite kit and leave the kids at home.

For nonvenomous snake bites, wound care is the same for other puncture wounds (see hook jabs, above).

SUN PROTECTION

In general, children receive three times the annual sun exposure of adults. Furthermore, most of one's lifetime sun exposure takes place in childhood. These facts have some pleasant connotations: that children spend a lot of time outdoors and presumably are having a good time doing so. However, there is a downside. Studies show that childhood is a particularly susceptible time for the cancer-producing effects of sunlight on the skin. And things aren't getting any better. Progressive depletion of the earth's protective ozone layer that normally filters out many of the damaging ultraviolet (UV) rays is expected to steadily increase the incidence of skin cancer. Although the word is out, it has not necessarily taken effect. One survey showed that although 90 percent of mothers associated skin cancer to overexposure to sunlight, only half of them regularly used sunscreens on themselves or their children.

Fly-fishing families must be particularly attentive to this problem, because light reflected from the water's surface is additive to direct exposure and may strike the skin in areas that might otherwise escape the sun's rays. Even if your family's time on the water is infrequent, protection is still needed. Although one type of skin cancer, basal cell carcinoma, is associated with cumulative sun exposure over time, another type, malignant melanoma, is related to short intermittent periods of intense exposure. Over the past 30 years, malignant melanoma has produced a greater incidence in mortality rate than any other cancer except lung cancer in women.

What should you do? Be sure everyone is wearing long-sleeved shirts, long pants, and brimmed hats. Dry clothing that is tightly knit blocks practically all UV radiation. You may want to drape a bandanna "foreign-legion" style from the child's hat down over the back of his head and neck. Use a waterproof sunscreen that is broad spectrum—i.e, that protects against UVA *and* UVB radiation, as both are harmful to the skin. The sunscreen should have a sun protection factor of at least 15. This number is the ratio of the time required to produce minimal redness of the skin with the sunscreen applied to the time required to produce the same amount of redness without the sunscreen. Kids tend to prefer the milky or gel type of sunscreens rather than those with an alcoholic base because the latter may burn or sting when applied.

Waiting for the skin to feel warm before you put on the sunscreen is too late. UVB, a particularly harmful form of ultraviolet radiation, does not produce a feeling of warmth unless the skin is already burned. Put on the sunscreen before you get to the water. Your application will be more careful (you will not be distracted by the rise forms) and you'll be more careful to avoid getting the sunscreen on your plastic fly line, which it might damage.

You may wish to add a physical sunscreen to the chemical sunscreens noted above. While the latter contain UV-light-absorbing chemicals, the former do not selectively absorb ultraviolet. Rather, they reflect and scatter light and prevent all solar radiation from reaching the skin. Zinc oxide is probably the most popular. This can be dabbed on selected areas such as the nose, lips, and the outer curve of the ears. Although it is visible and somewhat messy, kids tend to go for some of the brightly colored preparations that are now available.

Sunscreens need to be reapplied after sweating, swimming, and toweling. Such reapplications do not extend the period of protection, they merely maintain it. Because of this, sunscreens should not be used to justify an increase in sun exposure. Doctors warn patients to avoid sun exposure during the most intense period—between 10 A.M. and 3 P.M. Anglers should not find this too onerous, since during the summer months, this is the period when the fish are least likely to be biting.

WEATHER

For the cold and wet days, a three-layered clothing system is advised. There should be an outer water-repellent shell, a middle layer of insulating material such as down or polyester fill, and an inner layer of breathable material such as cotton. Add a hat and some gloves. If you've never tried this system before you will be amazed how well it works.

For the hot days you will naturally dress the kids in lightweight clothing but don't forgo the long-sleeved shirts and long pants to avoid not only the sun exposure but also the insect bites and the hook jabs.

A weather eye is one of the fly-fisherman's greatest assets. Not only can he rely on it to tell him when the fish are biting, it will also tell him when to get his butt off the stream. Many anglers are unaware that graphite fly rods attract lightning. Some manufacturers put warnings to this effect on their rods. If you and the kids find yourselves in a storm, get off the water immediately and lay down your rods. If you've got access to a hard-topped car, get inside it. Don't get into a convertible. If you can get into a house or cabin, stay away from open windows, doors, and the fireplace. Keep off the phone, unplug the television, and avoid water (faucets, sinks, bathtubs, and the like). If you're outside and do not have access to shelter, avoid tall trees, open fields, hilltops, and large metal structures such as flag and utility poles, and metal objects such as metal-framed backpacks and fences. A clump of short trees is a good destination. If you're caught in an open field, kneel or squat to limit your contact points with the ground—do not lie flat or stand.

These, then, are some of the principal safety issues when fly-fishing with children. The list is by no means inclusive. When you think about all of these issues at one sitting it can even make fly-fishing sort of scary. And some of the precautions may at times seem burdensome. But the excitement of catching fish on a fly rod is worth the extra time these precautions demand, especially if you're sharing that excitement with your children.

CHAPTER SIX

THE BUGS

If you know a child who has had the good fortune to attend a fly-fishing camp, ask him what part of the experience he liked the best. Chances are he'll say, "The bugs" (fig. 6.1). Maybe it's because latency-age children have an innate penchant for things creepy and crawly. Or perhaps their lifting nymphs from the dark recesses of a streambed reminds them of opening a present. Then again, catching bugs is a whole lot easier than catching fish. In any case, seining for insects is likely to bring cries of wonder and delight, and not only from the kids.

I recall the first time my fishing buddy Ted Rosenkrantz and I kicked up some stones in the Willowemoc Creek. We were attending an adult environmental education weekend at the Catskill Fly Fishing Center, and the instructor had handed us a rigid metal seine the size of a snowplow. A single pass of the seine through the water promptly told us that this place was a veritable bug factory. Our bounty included mayfly and stonefly nymphs, cased and uncased caddis larvae, hellgrammites, minnows, crayfish, and a host of additional creatures that defied identification. What surprised us as much as the catch was our reaction: We found ourselves whooping and hollering like children. At first we were chagrined by our involuntary outburst, but then we realized that the other adults were behaving in like manner. One thing was certain, none of us was thinking about taxes, unpaid bills, or deadlines on that occasion.

If I were president, I'd pass a law that requires every parent to take his child on a stream entomology tour at least once a year. If that sounds extreme, try it with your youngster and see what I mean. It's impossible

Fig. 6.1. A bug safari conducted by the Catskill Fly Fishing Center on the fabled Willowemoc Creek.

not to feel close to your child when the two of you are sharing such an exciting natural discovery. We'll devote this chapter to different ways of encountering the bugs, and we'll also comment on how to get help in understanding them if, like most of us, you do not secretly aspire to become a professional entomologist. Fortunately, getting into the bugs is a lot less expensive than getting into fly-fishing. A list of essential equipment is listed in table 6.1.

KICK SEINING

Inspecting the underside of rocks is the simplest way to go bug hunting and will be the method of choice for most of your outings. There are other times, particularly if your family is part of a team conducting a stream survey (see below), that more generous sampling is desired. This is where kick seining comes in. However, a word of caution is in order. Excessive kick seining—that done by large numbers of children repeatedly on a given stretch of water—can physically damage the streambed. So if your family pursues this activity be sure that it is permitted on your adopted stream and if so, exercise judgment and don't overdo it. Such moderation should not diminish the excitement and revelations that kick seining provides.

To seine properly, you'll need a screen with a sizable surface area—say three by three feet. Those tiny aquarium nets and pocket seines are inadequate. You can fashion your own seine by attaching a large swatch of flexible nylon or fiberglass screening (available in most hardware stores) to two stout wooden dowels (fig. 6.2). Binding the edges of the screen with a fold of duct tape or sewn canvas will help prevent fraying. If you want to get a very durable seine, you can purchase the Save Our Streams Kick Seine Net from Nichols Net and Twine Company, Inc., 2200 Highway 111, Granite City, Illinois 62040. It is $19.75 as of this writing, dowels not included, with discounts provided for more than one net.

Thus equipped, the first order of business is to pick out a buggy stretch of water. In general, riffles hold more aquatic insects than pools or runs because the water is more oxygenated. So select a shallow riffle where the current is not so fast that it will cause your kids to topple over. Face upstream and plunge the seine into the water so that the edge of the

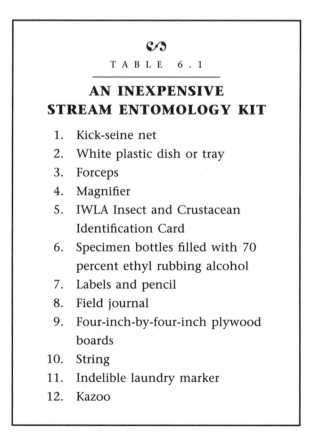

Table 6.1

AN INEXPENSIVE STREAM ENTOMOLOGY KIT

1. Kick-seine net
2. White plastic dish or tray
3. Forceps
4. Magnifier
5. IWLA Insect and Crustacean Identification Card
6. Specimen bottles filled with 70 percent ethyl rubbing alcohol
7. Labels and pencil
8. Field journal
9. Four-inch-by-four-inch plywood boards
10. String
11. Indelible laundry marker
12. Kazoo

Fig. 6.2. Left: A homemade kick-seine net. Right: Christopher identifies a mayfly nymph among the streambed fauna.

screen is flush with the streambed. Now ask the kids to position themselves upstream of the seine and dance around, thus kicking up the streambed stones (they should be wearing their felt-soled sneakers—chapter 2). At this point a little singing or other musical accompaniment helps. This is why I carry a kazoo in my fishing vest, a mystery my adult fishing companions have not fathomed. After a few minutes of this sort of thing, carefully raise the seine to avoid spilling the insects that have washed against its surface. One of your children may assist you by grasping the lower edge of the seine as you lift up the dowels.

Now bring the seine to the bank of the stream and transfer its contents into a white-bottomed tray that contains some stream water. We use an old, white dinner dish with a raised lip. The white surface sets off the bugs in striking relief, and the water will keep them alive for a short time. Here is where I must digress into my diatribe about cased caddis larvae. The cases are simply gorgeous, especially the ones made of tiny pebbles interlocked into an exquisite mosaic. It galls me to see anglers crushing the cases to squeeze out the larvae. All you have to do is leave the caddis in the examining tray. The oxygen supply of the water in the tray will be quickly expended, and in short order the larva will venture out of its case looking for more. At this point you can briefly inspect it, make any notations you require, and then restore both the insect and its home to the streambed. The larva deserves to eat plankton, get fat, and ultimately wind up in a trout's stomach, not in a gooey mess on your hands. For like reason, we release all of the bugs we capture, except for the few representative samples the children preserve in vials of 70 percent ethyl rubbing alcohol for study at home, in their science class, or at their scout meetings. Incidentally, if your child is a fly-tier (chapter 8) and is also looking for a grand idea for a science project, suggest that he tie imitations of the various insects he has collected and display them next to the preserved specimens. Call me if his teacher fails to grant him anything less than an A+!

THE BUG SANDWICH

What if you don't live near a stream as productive as the Willowemoc, and the insect harvest on your home stream is embarrassingly scanty? First, become an activist and get the stream cleaned up (chapter 10) and second, while this is in progress, treat your kids to an (inedible) bug sandwich. I first learned of this technique from Richard D. Klein's manual *Hands on Streams and Rivers* issued by the Maryland Department of Natural Resources' Save Our Streams Program. This is an effective way to obtain a concentrated sample of insects from an otherwise sparsely populated stream. The trick is to extend the collection period over weeks or months. Fortunately, you and your children do not have to be physically present during this entire period to realize the benefits of the method. Here's how it's done.

Cut out two pieces of plywood, each about the size of a piece of bread. Now ask your son to collect a bunch of freshly fallen leaves. He then sandwiches several inches of these leaves between the two pieces of plywood. Using an indelible laundry marker he writes his name as well as the date of the project on the outside of one of the plywood pieces. Next, he ties string around the sandwich to keep it from falling apart, and lashes the sandwich to a heavy rock to anchor it to the stream bottom. In four to six weeks, he returns to claim his prize. He opens the sandwich over a large white pan or dish to inspect the number and variety of aquatic insects that have decided to come and enjoy the meal.

BUG IDENTIFICATION

Unlike their angling parents, kids see no need to impress their peers with Latin terminology. This is yet another proof of the infinite wisdom of the young. If my boy said to me, "Look, Dad, an *Ephemerella subvaria*," I'd

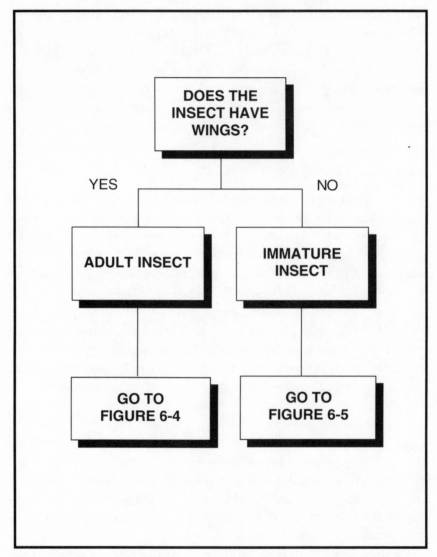

Fig. 6.3. The first step in identifying aquatic insects is to distinguish the grown-ups from the youngsters.

croak. Nonetheless, a little basic entomology will do them no harm, so I try to slip in a little now and then (see the Road Quizzes, appendix A). Identification of genera and species is hard enough for most adults, but identification at the order level is a realistic goal for most children. There are many orders of aquatic insects, but you can simplify things even further by just concentrating on the five most important ones: mayflies,

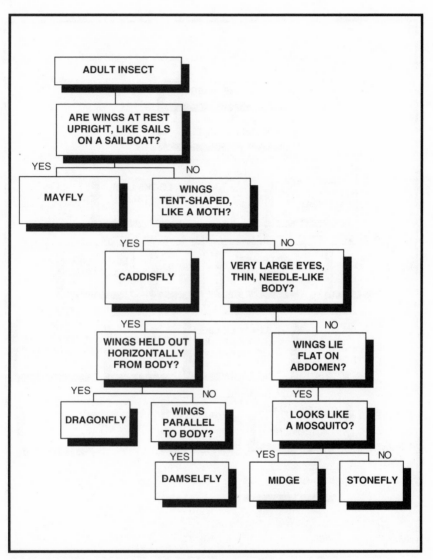

Fig. 6.4. Identifying the adults is fairly easy.

caddisflies, stoneflies, damsel/dragonflies, and the midges. The flow diagrams depicted in figs. 6.3, 6.4, and 6.5 provide a reasonable starting
point. As you can see, identification of adult insects depends primarily
upon the attitude of the wings at rest, while identification of the nymphs
relies heavily on the presence, type, and placement of gills. Like most flow
diagrams, these suffer from some oversimplification, for there are numerous other field marks that are too helpful to pass over. For instance,

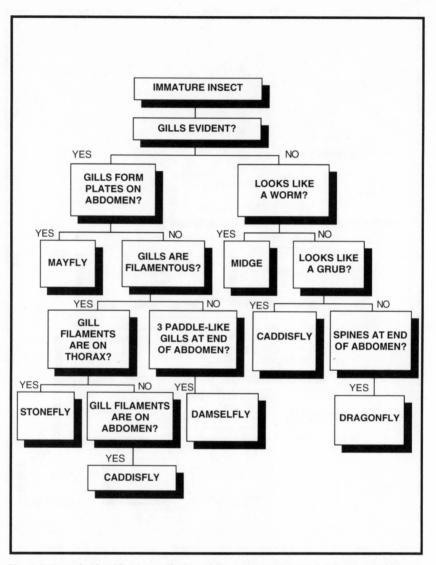

Fig. 6.5. Nymph identification calls for a lot more attention to detail. A magnifying device of some sort is a big help. Note that some but not all caddis larvae have readily identifiable gills, which accounts for their appearance on two separate limbs of the decision-making tree.

stonefly nymphs abide by the rule of two's: two antennae, two pair of wing cases, two claws on each foot, and two stiff tails. To delve into this further, pick up a copy of Marvin Nolte's *An Introduction to Aquatic Insects*, available for a song from the Federation of Fly Fishers. Also, be sure that your kids can get a magnified view of the insect. Although an ordinary hand lens will do, my children are partial to the two-way microscope, such as the one shown in fig. 6.6. This inexpensive gizmo, which is recommended for children six years of age and older, has a clear plastic observation tray with a raised edge to hold sufficient stream water to keep the insect happy and mobile. A magnifying lens at the apex of an over-lying pyramid is used to view the back of the insect, while a lens underneath the tray is aligned with an inclined mirror, permitting inspection of the insect's underside. (To avoid eye injury, the microscope should not be used in open sunlight—choose instead an area that is uniformly shaded or has some other cover. As with all magnifying devices, children should be carefully instructed never to look at the sun through either of the lenses.) My kids have made hard use of this device for over three years now, and it's still working fine. (Two-way microscopes are distributed in the U.S. by Battat, Inc., 2 Industrial Boulevard, West Circle, Plattsburgh, New York, 12901, and in Canada by Maison Joseph Battat, Ltd., 8440 Darnley Road, Montréal, Québec H4T 1M4.)

One of the invariable perplexities of being an amateur stream ento-mologist is that you come across bugs whose names have you stumped. If you don't mind carrying the extra bulk, field guides may be helpful, but we prefer to carry the eminently more portable *Identification Card for Stream Insects and Crustaceans* issued by the Izaak Walton League of America (chapter 7). This remarkable card encapsulates all the basic information required of the young naturalist, including whether a particular organism

MICHAEL McCARTER PHOTOS

Fig. 6.6. The photograph on the left shows the components of a two-way microscope: a vewing dome with a magnifier at its apex (left), an inspection tray (right), and a base that allows examination of the insect's underside (middle). The photograph on the right shows the assembled scope.

reflects the presence of clean, fairly clean, or polluted waters. These important relationships will be discussed in chapter 10.

Ultimately your child will be able to recognize a bug simply by glancing at it, without concentrating on the individual field marks, just as he can instantly recognize his Aunt Edna when she unexpectedly turns up for dinner. This will be your signal that he's ready for a more comprehensive study of stream entomology, and the two of you can elect to take on the aquatic moths and beetles, water bugs, alderflies, and dobsonflies.

Fig. 6.7. The SeaView Underwater Viewer.

FLAGRANTE DELICTO

One thing that observing an insect in a tray does not tell you is how it carries on its A.O.D.L. (Activities of Daily Living). The truly insatiable naturalist wants to know not only what the bug looks like, but also how it adapts to its environment. Your kids can ascend to this higher plane of observation without resorting to scuba gear, snorkeling or, heaven forbid, a glass-bottomed drift boat. The means of doing so is the SeaView Underwater Viewer, produced by Basic Designs, Inc., 5818 Bennett Valley Road, Santa Rosa, California 95404 and available in Canada from Outbound Products, 8585 Fraser Street, Vancouver, British Columbia V5X 3Y1 (fig. 6.7). This is an inflatable device with a flexible lens that provides a "zoom" effect when examining the stream bottom. The kids will put it to best use when wading quiet pools. With care they can also use it when drifting in a boat with you. Deflation of the SeaView permits easy storage and transport.

There's really no end to the number of fascinating subsurface high jinx of aquatic insects. For example, you may wish to direct your kids' attention to an uncased caddis larva spinning a net to catch the food drifting by; a cased caddis building its home; a caddis pupa rocketing to the surface with its trapped air bubbles; mayfly nymphs distinguishing themselves by their behavior (clingers, crawlers, burrowers, and swimmers), and, the pièce de résistance, a major insect hatch viewed from beneath the surface.

THE CLUBS

Sociologists tell us that man by nature is a joiner, and when I look at the contents of my mailbox, I know that they are right. If I enrolled in every organization that uses the postal service to solicit my membership, there would be scarcely money left to put food on the table, much less keep the kids in Reeboks. So some selectivity is in order, and when I look into the mailbox, I feel like a wary brown facing upstream, deciding where to take a bite. Since I am an avid angler, fishing organizations eclipse all the others, especially if they have an environmental bent and espouse an interest in children. Herewith is my top half-dozen.

TROUT UNLIMITED

1500 Wilson Boulevard, Arlington, Virginia 22209
Tel. 703-522-0200
and

TROUT UNLIMITED CANADA

P.O. Box 6270, Station D, Calgary, Alberta T2P 2C8, Canada
Tel. 403-221-8360

Trout Unlimited, although not limited to fly-fishers, has a rich legacy of conservation advocacy. As a student member, your child will receive a color decal, personal membership card, and a one-year subscription to *Trout* magazine. This quarterly periodical has a department entitled "For Small Fry" that consists of an illustration accompanied by some useful information about the natural history of trout or salmon. These articles are worth clipping and saving in a binder for your child to return to as needed.

Local TU chapters award special youth patches and decals to children who acquire fly-fishing and conservation skills under their aegis. Parents who want to learn how to become instructors may purchase TU's *Youth Education Handbook* for a nominal fee, and ask their chapter leaders for copies of *The Emerger*, TU's newsletter on youth education. The organization also provides a resource bibliography that will give you lots of ideas for developing an aquatic education curriculum directed toward children.

Trout Unlimited Canada is administered separately from TU in the United States, but its principles and goals are similar. Youth membership, available to those 17 years of age and younger, includes a decal, membership card, and a subscription to the quarterly magazine *Trout Canada*. Young members have been enthusiastically participating in the nationwide Yellow Fish Road Program by painting yellow fish symbols next to curbside storm drains. The symbols remind citizens that unwanted household products such as pesticides, oil, and cleaning agents should not be dumped into the drains. Unlike sanitary sewer systems that conduct raw sewage from homes and factories to treatment plants, storm sewer systems pass runoff directly into streams and creeks. Hence, pouring pollutants into storm drains can harm fish and other aquatic life, contaminate drinking water, and rob waterways of their recreational potential. Over a three-year period it is expected that all of Calgary's 40,0000 drains will be so marked. The general manager of TU Canada reports that many private-sector institutions have been impressed with the program's success in reducing pollution and have requested that their own drains be marked.

FEDERATION OF FLY FISHERS

P.O. Box 1595, 502 South 19th, Bozeman, Montana 59771
Tel. 406-585-7592

The FFF was founded almost 30 years ago by a small group of fly-fishermen and has since grown to include thousands of members and nearly 300 member clubs in the United States and Canada. Like TU, the annual student membership is inexpensive. It provides a cloth patch, decal, and sticker with the organization's logo, a membership card, and a subscription to the quarterly newsletter, *The F.F.F. Quill*. Request a copy of *Introduction to Fly Fishing*, a volume whose slender size belies its wealth of information. Other books offered, some for a nominal fee, include *Introduction to Aquatic Insects*, *Essentials of Fly Casting*, and *Catch and Release*. These should all be in every serious fly-fisher's library.

One of the distinct advantages of membership in the FFF is access to their audiovisual holdings. Tapes, film, and video cassettes are loaned by mail free of charge, with the member responsible for paying only return postage and insurance. A booklet of their items is available on request.

Student members are eligible to attend Youth Conclaves that are held in conjunction with regional and international meetings. At a recent Youth Conclave in Calgary, the FFF renewed its commitment to children. One of the outcomes is *The Junior Fly Fisher's Journal*. The *Journal* is America's first fishing publication exclusively for children. It is a quarterly that concentrates on fly-fishing education as well as the conservation and preservation of fish and water resources. It is included in the annual student membership fee.

Since most children find that panfish provide their entry point into the world of fly-fishing, it's fortunate that the FFF has established a Warm Water Committee. Committee members of the Northeast Council publish *The Hydrilla*, a newsletter that serves as a base of warmwater information, including fly patterns and fishing strategies. We panfish aficionados can now rest assured that we have achieved proper recognition within the fly-fishing fraternity since the Warm Water Committee has issued its own pins, hats, T- and sweat shirts.

THE IZAAK WALTON LEAGUE OF AMERICA

1401 Wilson Blvd. Level B, Arlington, Virginia 22209
Tel. 703-528-1818

The IWLA has been around since 1922 when a bunch of fishermen got together to help out the Mississippi River. It is a nonprofit organization whose 53,000 members promote citizen involvement in environmental protection and alert the public about emerging threats to natural resources. Although the league's strongest representation is in the Midwest, its activities and instructional materials are of interest to anglers nationwide. The league's flagship effort is the S.O.S. (Save Our Streams) Program that teaches individuals how to sample, identify, and record a stream's aquatic life to determine water quality, and also how to "adopt a stream" and become its active guardian (see chapter 10). Children will find much

Fig. 7.1. Every fly-fishing family deserves to make a pilgrimage here.

of the S.O.S. material extremely useful, including the *Insect and Crustacean Identification Card*, *The Save Our Streams* video, *The Stream Watchers Stream Guide*, and the brochures *Activities for Kids* and *Student Project Ideas*.

The organization sponsors the Uncle Ike Youth Education Program that aims to build a group of strong conservation leaders for the future. If you are interested in starting a similar program in your neighborhood, ask the IWLA to send you their booklet *Meet Uncle Ike: Chapter Guide to a Youth Education Program*.

Student membership is a bargain, and includes membership card, decal, and a subscription to the quarterly *Outdoor America* magazine.

THE CATSKILL FLY FISHING CENTER AND MUSEUM

R.D. #1, Box 130C, Livingston Manor, New York 12758
Tel. 914-439-4810

This is the organization that really opened up the world of fly-fishing for my children. The center (fig. 7.1) is located in the heart of the Catskill mountains, the birthplace of American fly-fishing, on the shores of one of its loveliest streams, the Willowemoc. Over the summer weekends, the center hosts eminently affordable environmental programs for children. Each weekend is designated for a particular age group, so you can be assured that your children will be with peers. You drop them off on Saturday morning and pick them up on Sunday afternoon. A sample of what goes on in between is shown in fig. 7.2. The cost is extremely reasonable and includes instruction, materials, use of fly-fishing tackle, lodging, and food. There are separate bunkhouses for girls and boys, and a counsellor is assigned to each bunkhouse to keep the lid on. Dinner is either in- or outdoors, depending on the weather, and desserts often consist of home-baked delectables brought in by the center's volunteers. This weekend has got to be one of the best things in the universe that you can give to a child.

I must confess to a sense of satisfaction that I felt when Amy first took the course in 1991. She was in esteemed company. Lee Wulff's nephew was a classmate and Poul Jorgensen was the guest fly-tier. This past season, both Chris and Amy took the course along with Ed van Put's nephews (a painting of the children along with their illustrious uncle hangs in the center's museum) and Harry Darbee's niece; Del Mezza was the guest tier.

The center's grounds are meticulously maintained. The stretch of river running through the property has been designated Wulff Run, and a visit to the commemorative plaque (fig. 7.3) is a good way to introduce your children to our fly-fishing heritage. Several Project Access points allow the handicapped access to the stream (see chapter 9). A lovely rain-fed casting pond is nearby, and instructors capitalize on this juxtaposition by encouraging the children to discover the many differences between pond and stream environments.

Catskill Fly Fishing Center and Museum

EDUCATIONAL PROGRAM
FOR GRADES 3–6

Saturday, July 10

9:30–10:30	Check-in
10:30–11:00	Orientation; camp rules; tour of grounds
11:00–12:00	Fish characteristics and types; demonstration of dissecting preserved fish specimen
12:00–1:00	Lunch/free time
1:00–1:30	Knot tying: how to tie on leaders and flies
1:30–2:00	Visit museum; watch guest fly-tier
2:00–3:30	Stream entomology
3:30–4:00	Snack
4:00–5:00	Rod setup; line and reel setup; casting practice
5:00–5:30	Stream safety
5:30–6:30	Dinner and cleanup
6:30–7:00	Nature walk
7:00–9:00	Basics of fly-tying and fly-tying practice
9:00–9:30	Video on trout
9:30–10:00	Camp fire
10:00	Lights out

Sunday, July 11

7:00	Wake-up
7:30–8:30	Breakfast and cleanup
8:30–10:00	Stream ecology; pond ecology temp; water testing: oxygen content, carbon dioxide content, acidity, etc.
10:00–10:30	Environmental games
10:30–11:30	Fishing
11:30-12:30	Lunch
12:30–1:00	Review
1:00–1:30	Camp cleanup
1:30–2:00	Pickup by parents

Fig. 7.2. A sample agenda from the Catskill Fly Fishing Center's environmental program for children

Fig. 7.3. The commemorative plaque at Wulff Run on the Willowemoc.

The center's museum holds a fascinating array of objects with sections devoted to such luminaries as Art Flick, Ed Zern, and of course Lee Wulff. Adult education programs are offered in the spring and they are planned as carefully as the children's programs. The casting club offers regular instruction on the pond, the litany of guest fly-tiers reads like a Who's Who in Fly-Fishing, and a flea market in August offers myriad delights, from tackle to ephemera.

There's no need to remain idle while your kids are at the center, because there's plenty of fishing nearby. After the major mayfly hatches are over in June, the area becomes more laid back. You can get up in the morning and actually find yourself alone in Hendrickson's Pool on the Beaverkill. The fish are still there, and they are plenty sophisticated. We're talking pillowlike presentations using long thin leaders on double-tapered fly lines. And at the end of the day you can still repair to the legendary Antrim Lodge for hearty portions of good food and fish talk.

FUTURE FISHERMAN FOUNDATION

1250 Grove Ave. Suite 300, Barrington, Illinois 60010

Tel. 708-381-4061

This nonprofit organization has developed a host of educational materials that are definitely worth obtaining. Although commonly used by schools, clubs, and other organizations, the materials are equally effective when used by families at home.

The foundation's major effort is to deliver one of the most important messages we can share with our children: "Get hooked on fishing, not on drugs." This nationally acclaimed program has justifiably won numerous accolades. It underscores the concept that fishing unites chil-

COURTESY FUTURE FISHERMAN FOUNDATION

Fig. 7.4. Some of the useful items offered by the Future Fisherman Foundation.

dren and parents by freeing them from the numerous daily distractions that they inevitably encounter.

The foundation can provide you with a variety of attractive, inexpensive items, including posters, brochures, bumper stickers, patches, decals, and videos that present fishing as a viable alternative to drug use (fig. 7.4). Placing these items at strategic locations around your home will help your kids know where you stand on these important issues. They also make great stocking stuffers on the holidays. And don't pass up the opportunity to offer your child the foundation's "First Fish Award" when she lands her first lunker of the day.

THE LOCAL CLUB

Although I could not hope to discuss all of the local organizations, personal experience allows me to expound enthusiastically about a sterling example, the Connecticut Fly Fishermen's Association (P.O. Box 380268, Silver Lane, East Hartford, Connecticut 06101; hotline telephone 203-664-3688). This group is so good you should consider joining it even if you don't live in Connecticut but are close enough to partake in some of the club's excellent activities. One of the most popular is the fly-fishing school directed by Gary Steinmiller. The course includes a total of 8 hours of didactic instruction, a half-day of casting practice on a private pond stocked with brookies, and a full day of angling on the fly-fishing-only stretch of the Willimantic River. During this last event, there is a one-to-one student-to-instructor ratio so that all major aspects of wading, casting, and presentation can be covered. The current cost for all of this is $40 for adult nonmembers, $30 for adult members, and $20 for youngsters. An extra $5 will get you a year's membership in the club. At these rates it's no wonder that students come from far and wide.

A telephone hotline is maintained to keep members informed of local fishing conditions, and the annual banquets feature speakers of international fly-fishing renown. The winter months are occupied by a rod-building school and courses in both introductory and advanced fly-tying. The tuitions are so reasonable you'd think you were in an earlier century. As with the fly-fishing school, the instructors are carefully selected for both their skill and teaching ability.

The club serves as primary steward for the fly-fishing-only stretch of the Willimantic. In fact, it was largely through the club's efforts that the once pollution-ridden stream was brought back to a viable fishery.

In reading this you may find parallels with your own local fishing club. Collectively, these grassroots groups can and do exert a tremendous influence on the future of our nation's waters. These waters are, of course, also our children's, and the clubs are excellent forums to sponsor youth education programs to ensure that our children's generation is not as hostile to streams and rivers as ours has been.

The CFFA's monthly meetings are open to all. There is no admission charge. Each meeting features fly-tying, a raffle, a lecture or demonstration on some aspect of fly-fishing, and coffee and doughnuts to follow. If you are in our neighborhood, come join us. Meeting times are announced on the hotline telephone number given above.

FLY-TYING

When I first began fly-fishing, I had some preconceived notions about tying flies. The first was that it was not for me. It seemed to require the persnickety kind of attention to detail that was beyond my reach. The second was that it was something only a select number of anglers could aspire to, given that there were so many more fly-fishers than fly-tiers.

These notions were shattered when I picked up Amy, then age nine, after her first weekend stay at the Catskill Fly Fishing Center, where she had participated in their environmental education program (chapter 7). She was bubbling over with enthusiasm about the friends she had made and the things she had done. I asked her if she thought she was ready for her first fly rod. She looked at me and said, "Dad, I'd rather have a fly-tying vise." She might as well have said, "Dad, I want to marry an extraterrestrial." I had narrowly assumed that since I had never been attracted to fly-tying, she wouldn't be either. Then she reached into her backpack and pulled out two respectably tied Woolly Worms. "Who did these?" I asked. "I did," she replied. "Who helped you?" I inquired. "Nobody really," she said, "I tied them myself after the instructor gave us a demonstration."

It took awhile for this news to settle in. By the time we had completed the three-hour drive back home to Connecticut, we had agreed that I would get her a vise and some materials. I mail ordered the items the next day, and they arrived a week later. While waiting, I felt myself getting interested in what might be in store. When the red-letter day came, she unwrapped the package, set up her tools, and proceeded to show me how to lock thread on the hook shank, tie in a tail, wrap chenille, palmer hackle, and tie a half-hitch finishing knot. The whole thing took her about four minutes. The adage that kids teach parents as much as parents teach kids suddenly seemed very relevant. As I admired her creation, she smiled and said, "Now it's your turn, Dad!" A few minutes later, I had finished my first Woolly Worm. It didn't look as nice as hers, but I thought it might look good to a fish someday, and sure enough it eventually did.

Since then our mutual hobby has blossomed. We have accrued an alarming array of tinsels, yarns, threads, and hackles, and have also taken the connoisseur's plunge: The simple beginner's vise has been replaced by a Renzetti, and we simply love it.

I now ruefully recall my early readings on fly-fishing, when I came upon Dave Whitlock's admonition that if a fly-fisher does not tie his own flies, he's missing out on at least 50 percent of the fun of the sport. Initially these words fell on deaf ears, but after Amy's first Catskill experience and her subsequent patient efforts in tutoring me, I can say unequivocally that Dave is right on target.

Initially Christopher showed a passing interest in the activity, but he did not exactly jump on the bandwagon. Then, last summer he was old enough to take the Catskill Fly Fishing Center course with Amy, who was returning for the second time. Since then he's been entirely gung ho about it. I'm not sure how the center's instructors manage to work such magic, but now that I've seen the favorable results in both of my children, I know that this is not fortuitous.

The children and I have shared wonderful times taking turns at the vise, delighting each other with fanciful creations that may never make the pages of a tackle catalogue, nor do all of them take fish. But none of us is losing any sleep over these matters.

From such inauspicious beginnings, fly-tying has become a personal obsession. Generally I'd rather have a few hours at the vise than go to a movie, a cocktail party, or shopping. If my children sit down and join me, it transcends the merely enjoyable and reaches the sublime. My singular regret is that I did not discover this rewarding activity at a much earlier age. If you have resisted the allure of fly-tying thus far, my only advice is to throw caution to the wind and forge ahead. Don't be intimidated by those practitioners who revel in their ability to produce #26 midges. Even if a #10 wet fly is the smallest thing your hands can turn out, your satisfaction will be no less. It's like learning a new language, only infinitely simpler. Once you learn the basic order of construction of four generic patterns—dry fly, wet fly, nymph, and streamer—you can tie almost anything, and you can teach your child to do the same. Suddenly, all of those fly-tying articles that seemed to needlessly take up so much space in your fishing magazines become vital communications addressed specifically to you. By just reading the ingredients for a particular fly pattern, you will know all the steps required to put them together. Sure there are the fine points, and one can devote an entire lifetime to learning them. But you don't have to be Van Cliburn to play Tchaikovsky, and fortunately fish don't have that discriminating an ear. Panfish, in fact, will listen to just about anything!

GETTING STARTED

If you are already a fly-tier, chances are you will not need to go out and buy a separate set of tools for junior. On the other hand, not everything you own may be suitable for him to use, and other items may become suitable if you are willing to modify them a bit. If he shows a real interest, he will ultimately ask for some personal equipment, for there is no denying the pride of ownership. So whether your closet is chock full of fly-tying materials, or you're just starting out in tandem with your child, here are some recommendations for selecting equipment.

HOOKS

The hook that seems to have been custom made for the young fly-tier is the size 8, 3X long, 1X strong, round bend, down-eye nymph hook. The hook is not so large that it will not be accommodated by standard vise jaws, nor is it so small that tying on fine or delicate materials becomes excessively cumbersome. It is ideal for Woolly Buggers, small streamers, and long-bodied nymphs. Once you buy a package, the first thing you should do is debarb all of the hooks. *In my opinion, there is absolutely no role for barbed hooks anywhere in the field of fishing with children.* Even if you do not subscribe to the catch-and-release philosophy, extracting a debarbed hook that has accidentally lodged under the skin of your child is a lot less painful and damaging than removing a barbed one (chapter 5).

Debarbing has become an art form in itself. This is out of necessity. Although barbless hooks occasionally can be found in stores and tackle

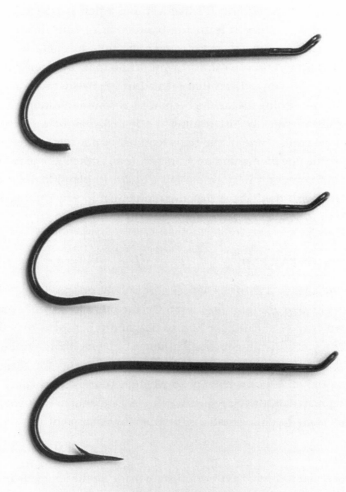

JOSEPH DRISCOLL PHOTO

Fig. 8.1. Top: Hook with point and barb removed is just right for beginning tiers. Middle: Debarbed hook with point intact is used after the child has demonstrated competence and safety at the vise. Bottom: Barbed hooks should not be used by children.

catalogues, they are sadly the exception rather than the rule. Let me share with you a debarbing method that works best for me. Take the hook and insert it upside down in the vise jaws. Now use a long-nose pliers with *flat* jaws to press the barb down. Notice that I said press, not crunch or mash. That's the beauty of the flat jaws. Unlike pliers with serrated jaws, they do not mangle the hook and thereby weaken it. For freshwater hooks, the Ace Hardware four-inch flat-nose Hobby Plier #24131 (Ace Hardware

Corporation, Oak Brook, Illinois 60621, fig. 8.2) just can't be beaten. Make sure that when debarbing you wear protective eyewear with sideshields. Even in the best of hands, the barb will occasionally zing off into the air. For this reason, make sure the kids are not around when you are debarbing. Eventually your children will move on to a greater variety of hook styles and sizes, but the need to debarb will always remain.

For the younger child and any other absolute beginner, an additional precaution should be taken. Use wire cutters to remove the entire point with its barb, and then machine down any rough burrs (fig. 8.1). Again the protective eyewear is needed. Alternatively, use the Touch And Go (TAG) hooks available from Partridge of Redditch, Redditch, Worcestershire B97 4JE, England. These have an extra eye in place of the point and barb. Now the child can't get jabbed regardless of whether the hook is in or out of the vise. Once she has gained some familiarity with tying, she can begin using debarbed hooks, but she should enclose the point of the hook within the jaws of the vise. Purists will note that this may weaken the hook, but better a few lost fish than an injured daughter. Only once your child gains full proficiency with her tools and consistently demonstrates care and safety in her tying should you permit her to use conventional hook placement with the point of the hook protruding from the jaws (fig. 8.3).

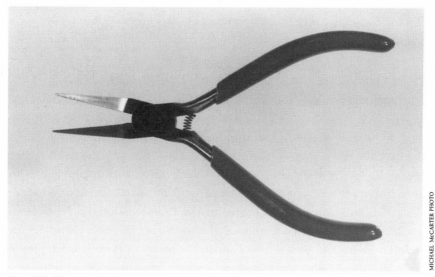

Fig. 8.2. The Ace Hardware four-inch Hobby Plier (model #24131) is excellent for debarbing freshwater hooks. Note the flat jaws.

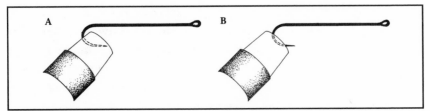

Fig. 8.3. a) Encasing the point of the hook within the vise jaws will help prevent accidental jabs. b) The conventional hook placement for more accomplished tiers.

VISE

The problem with cheap vises is that they simply don't do their job: hold the hook securely. This can create safety problems if your child is putting a lot of tension on the tying thread. A few extra dollars will get you something reliable. The industry standard for years has been the Thompson Model A, a tool that is inspiring to use. It is the same vise that Catskill-legend Harry Darbee tied on, and people came from all over the world for his flies! Among the fancy vises, if you can afford a true rotary model, like the Renzetti Traveller, go for it. Kids have no more difficulty learning to use a rotary vise than do adults, and they will equally appreciate the advantages. Although many commercial fly-tiers prefer vises with spring-loaded jaws because hook changing is quick, they are not suitable for children: Little hands cannot squeeze the release lever hard enough to open the jaws. Finally, be sure to get a clamp rather than a pedestal-type vise. The former are not only cheaper, they are much more stable on the work surface.

THREAD

6/0 prewaxed nylon is the workhorse of the profession. In the hands of experienced tiers, it affords the near-perfect compromise between thickness, to provide strength, and thinness, to avoid bulk. Unfortunately, in the hands of the young tier just starting out, the thread is too delicate and break-offs are frustratingly common. The solution to this problem is to use a heavier thread. For the panfish patterns most children start off with, the added bulk will not be a problem. The thread I strongly recommend is a 2/0 braided nylon made on special order by the Danville Company for S&M Fly Tying, 95 Union Street, Bristol, Connecticut 06010, telephone 203-589-1844. The thread is not only sturdy, it's very inexpensive.

Fig. 8.4. Fly-tying scissors typically have extremely sharp points (left). For children's use, the points should be machined smooth (right).

SCISSORS

High-quality fly-tying scissors are a joy to use. They are machined to extremely close tolerances and will help make your kids' flies look great. The one problem is that the blades taper to very fine points. Needlelike is not too strong a designation. This is to facilitate delicate work, as in trimming Catskill-style dry flies. In children's hands, the scissors are just too risky as they are, so I recommend that the tips be ground down (fig. 8.4). The cutting edges along the shafts of the blades will continue to do an excellent job, and for most of the panfish patterns that your child will be tying, the loss of the tips will not be missed. One does not need surgical-quality scissors to cut rubber legs for a Foam Cricket, for example.

Which reminds me. Discourage your children from using fly-tying scissors for cutting coarse, stiff or hard materials, such as deer hair, duck quills, and metal ribbing wire. A second, less expensive pair of all-purpose scissors should be set aside for these jobs. Color coding the handles of the scissors with a dab of paint may assist their choosing the correct one.

BOBBIN

For a bobbin, there is only one choice. It's the S&M model with the short tube (fig. 8.5). Why is this item so outstanding? Well, remember when you were a youngster and you were first learning to write? The teacher gave you one of those pencils as fat as a cigar so you could get a good grip on it, and you were happy because it made things easier for you. The S&M has a nice, chunky base that your kids can get a handle on, the short tube allows them to get closer to their work, and the tube is machined so that thread break-offs rarely if ever occur. If that isn't enough, the modest price of the bobbin includes a spool of that special Danville thread I was talking about. I remember the first time I brought home one of these bobbins for my daughter. It looked so unlike any of her conventional wire bobbins, she wasn't completely sure what it was. But after she tried it out the first time, she became an instant convert. She's become quite selective about this and now refuses to use any of the old wire bobbins.

BODKIN

This tool is used to pick out dubbing material, separate hackle fibers, and perform so many other tasks that it is truly one of the fly-tier's indispensable items. The problem I faced was that I did not want my children

Fig. 8.5. The S&M Bobbin.

playing with metal needles (watching how they handled barbless hooks was consuming enough of my attention). So, I compromised. Toothpicks work almost as well and are a lot safer.

HACKLE PLIERS
Having hackle repeatedly slip from the jaws of the pliers is the bane of the profession. Save your kids much of the agony by getting a pair of rubber-tipped hackle pliers. Despite published controversy over this matter, I've found that they really do help.

HALF-HITCH TOOL
The tip section of a ballpoint pen with the refill removed is all the kids will need (fig. 8.6). Using this tool is much easier than tying a manual half-hitch and light years easier than tying a whip-finish knot.

HEAD CEMENT
If your children can tie decent half-hitches, they do not really need to finish off the heads of their flies with cement. This is just as well, because the stuff is gooey, hard to clean up, volatile, and poisonous. On those rare occasions when the head of the fly really calls for some cement, I will closely supervise their using my preferred finishing cement—lady's nail hardener available at the cosmetics counter of your department store or pharmacy.

PIN-BACKS, EARRING HOOKS, AND TIE TACKS
Although not traditional parts of the fly-tier's armamentarium, these items, available in any craft store, will extend the range of your child's fly-tying activities (fig. 8.7). This is especially true for girl tiers. I've supplied Amy with hooks that have points and barbs removed and all rough burrs machined down. The pointless and barbless TAG hooks by Partridge are also suberb for this purpose. She has used them to tie quite a variety of wet-fly earrings and streamer brooches (fig. 8.8). These have created quite a stir at her school and over the past few months she's tied a number of them for her friends.

FLY-TYING MATERIALS
Bad materials take all the fun out of fly-tying because they are hard to work with. I'm not suggesting that you go out and buy your son a pile of

grade #1 genetic dry-fly necks. Materials that good are ecstasy to use but hard on the wallet. For this reason, my kids and I have stayed away from dry-fly work and concentrate almost exclusively on wet flies, nymphs, and

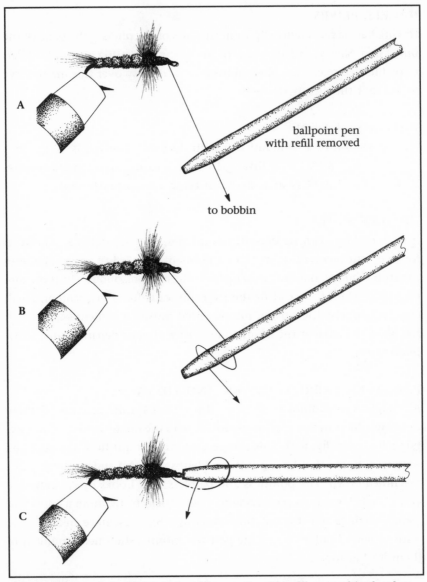

Fig. 8.6. The pen-tip half-hitch tool. a) The pen tip with refill removed is placed on top of the tying thread. b) The tying thread is looped around the pen tip. c) The opening of the pen tip is placed over the eye of the hook and the loop of thread is slid onto the head of the fly and tightened.

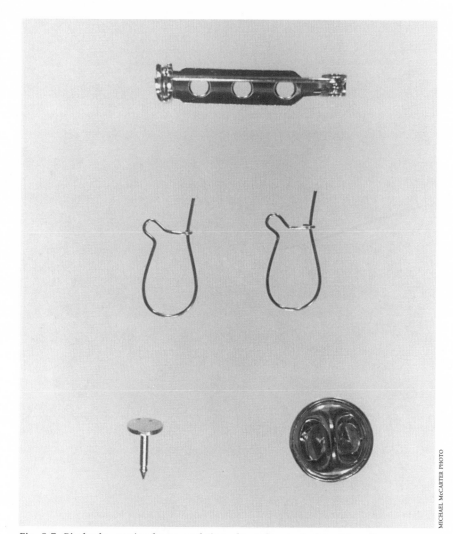

Fig. 8.7. *Pin-backs, earring loops, and tie tacks make wonderful settings for your children's flies. Hook barbs and points should be removed and any rough burrs sanded smooth before mounting.*

streamers. For $1.50 I bought enough first-quality grouse feathers to keep us in soft-hackled wet flies until the cows come home. A grade #2 Metz grizzly rooster saddle, purchased for less than $10 two years ago, will continue to provide us with hackle for Woolly Worms for many more years to come. We've found that synthetic yarns purchased from our local department store are available in an unbelievable variety of colors and diameters, and substitute nicely for dubbed bodies. The hardware store

Fig. 8.8. A young fly-fisher wears earrings of her own creation.

keeps us supplied with thin silver, gold, and copper wire for sturdy ribbing material. Fabric and craft stores have proven a fertile source of a wide variety of body and winging materials (fig. 8.9). Then of course there is the fly shop, our destination on so many rainy afternoons, a place where your imagination (and your checkbook) can run wild.

Although the most economical approach is to buy only those materials that will be used for specific patterns, to deny the children leeway to pick out what captures their fancy is to pass up a wonderful opportunity for them to exercise their creativity. When we enter the fly shop, my kids instantly gravitate to the materials that sparkle or are fluorescent. The results have been intriguing, both to me and, occasionally, to a hefty bass.

INSTRUCTION BOOK

Dick Stewart's *Universal Fly Tying Guide* (Mountain Pond Publishing, North Conway, New Hampshire, 1994, distributed by The Countryman Press, Woodstock, Vermont) is like a work by Hemingway: spare, meaningful, and filled with vivid images. This book did not win the Book of the Year award from the United Fly Tiers for nothing. The beginning of the book clearly illustrates the steps necessary to create the four generic patterns described earlier in this chapter, and the splendid photographs that follow will guide your child through the specific recipes. This book is more valuable than many fly-tying manuals costing a great deal more.

INSTRUCTIONAL VIDEO

As stated in chapter 4, the Orvis Company's production *Save A Worm—Tie A Fly* is the premier choice.

FLY-TYING KITS

Generally I don't recommend prepackaged fly-tying kits. The instruments are frequently flimsy, and the materials tend to be of poor quality and hastily assembled with no particular patterns in mind. A notable exception is the Orvis Fly Tying Kit for Kids. The vise and other tools are sturdy and well machined, and the materials are all top drawer. The kit contains all of the materials needed to tie caterpillar, spider, minnow, and dragonfly imitations. The instructions are extremely precise and well illustrated,

JOSEPH DRISCOLL PHOTO

Fig. 8.9. Items garnered at craft stores and fabric outlets make excellent fly-tying materials.

so you need not fear that you will be unable to adequately guide your child if you have not had any fly-tying experience. An added benefit is that part of the proceeds from the sale of these kits is donated to summer programs for seriously ill children.

THINGS YOUR CHILD DOESN'T NEED
Dubbing twisters, hackle guards, hair stackers, wing burners, wing dividers, fur blenders, and whip-finishing tools all have their place, and in time your child may grow to need them. But for now, the essential items I've listed above will keep him more than occupied.

BEYOND THE VISE

The past few pages have dealt primarily with the technical aspects of fly-tying. Far more important are the spiritual aspects. Not too long ago I came across an article in *The New York Times Magazine* by Craig Nova, a novelist who lives in Vermont. To me, he seemed to say it better than anyone. It is reprinted here in its entirety.

TIES OF AFFECTION
Recently I have been teaching my 12-year-old daughter how to do some fly-fishing. Mostly this is something that is enjoyable and safe, but there are certain parts that, while obviously dangerous, still don't reveal their secrets until you've had a bad moment.

For instance, some years ago I was fishing on the White River in Vermont (where I live). The water was high, but I was wading in it, and while I had been taught that you should never wade downstream in heavy water, somehow (probably because it had never really been impressed upon me) I disregarded this rule. I stepped into the head of a pool, which was deep. I went down far enough for the water to come up to my chest and even to come over the tops of my waders. I turned around and faced upstream and immediately saw my predicament: I could not go back the way I had come because the weight of the current was too much, and yet downstream the water was even deeper, over my head. There was nothing to do but swim for it, keeping an eye on the boulders that stuck out of the greenish water of spring. So, I'm careful about what I teach my daughter, especially when it comes to hidden danger.

We began with casting, starting out on the lawn with a bit of yarn instead of a fly, and even when we went to a pond up the road and I tied on a Royal Coachman, I broke off the barb of the hook. It didn't take long before she could handle a fair amount of line. There are other things that go into catching trout aside from wading and casting, and in the winter, I have been showing her how to tie flies too. During one of these times, when I was getting ready to tie a fly, my daughter said to me, "What's it like to be in love?"

She said this with the same frankness she might have used in asking when white mayflies appear on the water. Mostly, she is not too interested in tying flies. I don't make a big deal out of trying to teach her—this part will probably come by itself in time. I show her some flies that I've tied, or sometimes she'll watch while I make preparations to tie flies. She asked about being in love when I was getting ready to tie a fly pattern called a Hendrickson.

In the early spring, a mayfly of this name appears on my favorite water. It has gray glassine wings, which remind me of silk stockings, and its body has a little purple in it, the same color as the vernal blush the trees have just before they begin to put out leaves. To get this color into the fly pattern I mix in a little purple fur with the imitation fox I use to make the body. I buy some Australian possum (domestically grown), and I dye a piece of it in a pot on the stove. I was on one side of the pot and she was on the other when she asked about love.

For a moment we looked at each other through the purple mist that rose from the pot. It seemed there was a sensation of being a "father" so definitely on my face as to feel like a mask, and more than anything else, I wanted to drop that and to be absolutely direct.

"There are all kinds of love," I said.

"Like what kinds?" she said.

"Well, you could be passionately in love," I said.

She looked at me, considering this. I immediately thought about how much, if at all, we should talk about AIDS. We have talked about it before. Now, though, it seemed best not to harp on it like some anxiety-stricken creature.

"Then there are other kinds of love too. You can love a friend. You can be married to someone for 50 years, and what you feel then might be different, even stronger than what you felt when you were first courting. There are all kinds."

This sounded a lot like a kind of counter on which endless varieties of love were displayed, like bolts of cloth, but I was stuck with it.

"Which kind is the best?" she said.

I looked into the pot, where the purple, faintly rolling surface was marked with foam that formed weblike shapes, just like the ones in the ocean after a wave breaks. I reached to the bottom with a long fork and picked out the fur. The dye ran off it, and we listened as it dripped back into the pot, the sound seeming to be a perfect combination of memories (on my part) and anticipation (on her part).

"That's hard to say," I said. "What do you think?"

"How would I know?" she said.

She stared right at me.

"Well?" she said. "I want the truth."

"It varies with how old you are," I said. "I like the kind that really lasts. But I guess you have to decide for yourself which you like best."

She looked at the wet, purple fur.

"What are you going to tie?" she said.

"Some Hendricksons," I said.

"Oh," she said. "We'll go fishing in the spring, won't we?"

"Sure," I said. "Yes. Of course. Yes. My darling."

But the discussion of love has somehow got mixed up with catching trout, and this combination has left me with a lot of questions. What is it I am really trying to convey to my daughter by teaching her the habits of mayflies, the times of their emergence from the stream, or how you recognize each variety of trout? This question is made concrete for me when I think about a particular piece of water I fish in the spring.

It is a long pool, deep along the bank, and at the head of it there is a run where the water passes over gravel. There is an apple tree on the bank, and in the spring, when the Hendricksons are on the water, the flowers of the tree are reflected on the surface of the glide. The fish rise to the mayflies, dimpling the water and sometimes making a splash, the fish showing themselves in a crown-shaped explosion of water as they fall back into the stream. Of course, I cast a fly to float over those places where the fish are rising.

On these spring afternoons, when I stand in this particular spot, I have forgotten my business (as much as possible) and for a while, when the fish are rising, it seems that I exist outside time, although in the midst of all this, there will be a memory of some kind, a bit of piercing intimacy. It is not that I am peaceful at this moment so much as comfortably alive and excited, although I feel something like humility too. I think about my dead father. I am alone, but not lonely at all.

This moment, I guess, is what I want to convey to my daughter. But how much of this will she take as her own, and will she understand that this was the thing I was trying not to teach but to give?

The fish I catch here are rainbows, wild fish, bright red on the sides, a little green on the back and with some spots, and the river valley is small, marked on both sides by hills of irregular shape, some of them bare and showing gray rock. I let the fish go now, carefully putting them back, since the pleasure is not so much in eating them anymore. I would like to think that one day my daughter might stand in this same spot and remember, as she makes her casts, those winter nights when we dyed fur and talked about love. She'll have her own memories by then. And, with any luck, in a moment of keen distraction, she'll see the rainbows rising along the bank.

C H A P T E R   N I N E

THE DISABLED CHILD

One crisp fall evening as I was shuffling through my mail, I came across a copy of the *Orvis News*. It contained an article by Tom Rosenbauer about how he and another fly-fisherman, Tom Earnhardt, visited actor Paul Newman's Hole in the Wall Camp in Connecticut. This camp provides outstanding recreational opportunities for children with cancer and other serious conditions. The two Toms taught the kids how to tie flies and, to make a long story short, the program was a resounding success. Encouraged by this experience, the Orvis Company, where Tom Rosenbauer works, agreed to produce a video specifically designed to teach kids how to tie flies (chapter 8). Tom's article indicated that Orvis was willing to supply the video and fly-tying equipment free of charge to the Child Life Programs of other hospitals.

The article was a real eye-opener. Although I had both tied flies and worked with handicapped children, I had never before envisioned a relationship between the two. I became so enthralled with the idea that I could not sleep that night. The next morning, I ran bleary-eyed into the Child Life Office of the Newington Children's Hospital, where I am on staff. I explained the program to the Child Life team, and they got nearly as excited as I was. Steve Balcanoff and Don Chaffee of the Department of Therapeutic Recreation were called in and they offered me their full support. I then put in a call to Tom Rosenbauer at Orvis. He was very pleased to hear of our interest, and promptly sent along the video, tools, and tying materials.

The next step was to assemble a cadre of instructors. At that month's meeting of the Connecticut Fly Fishermen's Association I asked for volunteers and instantly got two dozen of them. The following week we all met at the Newington Children's Hospital to discuss strategy over coffee and pastries. The amount of energy and interest was terrific, but would we be able to communicate our enthusiasm to the kids?

Our maiden voyage was Teen Weekend. This is a time that the hospital sets aside to provide vocational counselling and recreational activities for teenagers with meningomyelocele. These children are born with a congenital abnormality of the spine that often results in partial or total paralysis below the waist. Thus we anticipated that most of the weekend's participants would be wheelchair bound but have reasonable facility with their hands. Our fly-tying would supplement the usual activities, such as jewelry making and wheelchair basketball.

Five instructors were assigned to the weekend. The teenagers' response was tentative at first, but after a few of them found out how easy it was to turn out a Woolly Worm, the word spread and enthusiasm accelerated, with some of the kids electing to tie five or six patterns during a single sitting (fig. 9.1).

Armed with this initial victory, we moved our activities to the inpatient psychiatric service at the Newington Children's Hospital. Although most of these patients do not suffer physical handicaps, they do

MICHAEL McCARTER PHOTO

Fig. 9.1. Veteran fly-fisherman Paul Brodeur (right) teaches patient Darren Anderson how to tie his first fly during Newington Children's Hospital Teen Weekend.

have social and/or emotional problems severe enough to warrant extended hospital stays. Here for the first time I became hesitant, for the behavior of some of these unfortunate children can be highly unpredictable. I shared my concern with the fly-tiers, but was overjoyed when they were not the least bit discouraged.

What happened next was extraordinary. The time and date were set, and as I went down from my office to the lobby to meet my fellow tiers, I was intercepted by a messenger who handed me a note hastily written by the head psychiatric nurse. It informed me that the day had been a disaster for the kids on the unit. Most had been oppositional and defiant, and many had to be resigned to "time out" in their rooms. The letter concluded sorrowfully that fly-tying would probably not go over well that evening.

I discussed this with the other instructors, and we decided to give it a go anyway. We divided into two groups. One would teach those children who could safely leave the ward. This would take place in a nearby conference room, and nursing supervision would be provided. The other group would enter the closed ward to teach those children whose behavior required them to remain behind. For safety reasons, the points and barbs were removed from all of the hooks ahead of time.

The results exceeded our highest expectations. The kids entered into the tying with gusto, they were extremely respectful of the instructors, and were obviously delighted with the individual attention they were getting (we planned for a one-to-one student-instructor ratio). Afterwards, they showed off their creations to one another with pride; their rush of self-esteem was almost palpable. We also had some typed fly-tying instructions for the kids. One child asked his instructor to sign the handout. This sparked other kids to request the same. In no time all of the instructors were signing each child's instructions and it looked like a night at the Oscars.

Those who entered the closed ward had similar success. One encounter is especially worth relating. When instructor Gary Bogli entered the room of a confined patient, the boy threw himself on the floor, buried his face in his arms, and refused to come to the table. Now Gary is skilled at dealing with this sort of thing because he teaches middle school. He simply took out his vise and began tying. The boy eventually looked up and could not overcome his own curiosity. When the boy walked over, Gary unceremoniously set up another vise. The boy sat down. There was a lengthy interval during which neither said a word as Gary's fly gradually took on form and substance. Then the boy looked up at Gary and said, "Show me." Two hours later, when it was time to close shop, the boy wanted Gary to stay and supervise his tying flies for every member of his family!

When all of the children were reassembled on the ward, the nurses were incredulous. The kids were calm and well behaved. After a pleasant snack, they all went peacefully to bed. It was as if their oppositional behavior earlier in the day had been a distant dream. I will not go so far as to say that fly-tying is a substitute for psychotherapy, or that it will work similar magic on every occasion. But the results of that evening were unmistakable, and 14 fly-tiers left the hospital that night feeling as uplifted and renewed as the children.

Lessons like these have taught me that the arts of fly-fishing are accessible to most children who are physically or emotionally disabled. For fly-tying, there are no necessary modifications other than those enumerated for children in general in chapter 8. For fly-fishing, a number of adjustments may be needed depending on the individual child's functional level. Let's look at some of them now.

ACCESS

It is a maxim that the largest fish reside in the most inaccessible locations. If you dwell on this a bit, you can probably think of at least a dozen biological reasons why this is so. What does this mean to the disabled child? That some of the loveliest and most productive waters are permanently off-limits to him. These children know that access is a two-edged word: When it is offered it is a tool for freedom and self-fulfillment; when it is withheld, it is tantamount to incarceration.

It is difficult for nondisabled individuals to fully comprehend this duality. I know of an especially enlightened professor of pediatrics who required his medical students to spend 24 hours confined to a wheelchair with no change in their usual academic and personal schedules. Their appreciation of what it means to be disabled was quickly brought into focus. The students found that things they'd never noticed, like the absence of bevelled curbs on street corners, were suddenly viewed as personal insults. So too with the impatience of others waiting behind them on the cafeteria line as they struggled with their trays and utensils.

And I need not belabor the difficulty each student encountered in at-tempting to transfer from wheelchair to toilet and back again.

Fortunately, many communities have become sensitive to these issues and have come up with tangible solutions ranging from the simple to the complex. Fig. 9.2 shows a lovely spot dedicated to the handicapped on the shore of Eastbury Pond in Glastonbury, Connecticut. The ap-proach is level without obstacles, there is ample room for a back cast, and a bannister provides support for the caster. More ornate is the casting platform at the Hemlocks, a camp sponsored by the Easter Seals for

Fig. 9.2. Fishing areas for the handicapped range from simple banisters, such as the one at Eastbury Pond in Glastonbury, Connecticut (top), to more elaborate facilities, such as the casting platform at The Hemlocks in Hebron, Connecticut (bottom).

Fig. 9.3. The handicapped access area on the fly-fishing-only stretch of the Salmon River in Colchester, Connecticut (top left) consists of switchbacks (top right) that gently slope to a pair of casting jetties (bottom).

handicapped children in Hebron, Connecticut. Here some fencing is installed beneath the bannister to prevent any wheelchair spills into the water. Such praiseworthy efforts are not confined to still waters. On the fly-fishing-only stretch of the Salmon River in Colchester, Connecticut, a series of switchbacks enables the handicapped to descend an otherwise steep bank and reach two casting jetties that project into some very productive water (fig. 9.3).

If your community lacks such structures there is a carefully considered way of correcting this deficiency. It's called Project Access, and you can reach them at P.O. Box 299, Village Station, New York, New York 10014. This program's mandate is to make productive fishing waters accessible to handicapped and elderly anglers. Their success has been impressive. A short time ago, for example, a group of local residents and sporting clubs volunteered their time and, using Project Access guidelines, created seven entry points on the Willowemoc and Beaverkill watersheds in the Catskill Mountains (fig. 9.4). The paths are adjacent to parking areas and lead to prime fishing waters. The surfaces of the paths consist of a mixture of clay, gravel, and sand. This settles firmly, resists weed overgrowth, and blends in naturally with the landscape. It also comfort-

Fig. 9.4. Project Access Points at Wulff Run (top) and Hazel Bridge (bottom) on the Willowemoc Creek.

ably supports wheelchair use even after a rainfall. The paths are level from side to side and descend no more than 12 inches for every 12 feet of length. When necessary, switchbacks have been used to guarantee the rate of descent. The paths are diverted around trees and shrubs to avoid uprooting, and shrubs and cuttings have been planted where necessary to stabilize the bank. Ongoing maintenance of the paths has been arranged with a local resident who checks them every other week.

Last year on our annual pilgrimage to the Catskills, my father, who is 79 years old, was able to comfortably reach the shores of Wulff Run on the Willowemoc by using one of the Project Access paths. Although we had made many trips to the stream before, this was the first time he was able to get close enough to the water to observe his grandchildrens' fledgling fly-fishing efforts. I can still sense his joy and appreciation of that day. Experiences such as these have made our family strong believers in the Project Access program.

The Project Access Committee will provide you with all the information you need to organize volunteers, select a site, and install materials. In addition to written instructions, a companion video highlights all of the major steps. According to Joan Stoliar, the program's principal organizer, the ultimate aim is to establish a network of accessible, productive fishing locations throughout the United States and Canada, coupled with a communications system that will permit the Project Access Committee to share this information with all interested sportsmen.

TECHNIQUES

All of the still-water techniques described in chapter 4 are applicable to the disabled child. Whether a child wades will depend on her particular abilities, but don't overlook fishing from the banks of streams and rivers. Remember again that the English have avoided wading for centuries and they, more than anyone else, are responsible for the sport as we know it today. Besides, most anglers know that they are usually wading through schools of shoreline fish on their way to the center of a pool.

Most fly-casting can be executed with facility from a wheelchair, and the lower profile offered by the seated position means that the angler is less likely to spook fish. For those handicapped children who do not possess the manual dexterity to handle a fly-rod, spin-casting a fly with a casting bubble may be just the thing (chapter 2). But before committing fully to this alternative, consider a number of helpful devices that may still make fly-rod mastery a realistic challenge for the child. These include rod holders, line threaders, automatic fly reels, fly boxes that can be operated with one hand, and various hand supports. For a comprehensive list of items, send for the catalogue *Products to Assist the Disabled Sportsman* distributed by J.L. Pachner Ltd., 13 Via Di Nola, Laguna Niguel, California 92677.

And if you're one of those parents who is equally at home in the workshop as on the stream, don't overlook the numerous devices that you can construct yourself. For instance, a short piece of hollowed dowel inserted over the handle of a single-action fly reel may assist the child in retrieving line. Attaching a lanyard between the fly rod and wheelchair will enable him to independently retrieve his rod if he mistakenly drops it. A bracket attached to a tackle box can be reversibly clamped to the arm of the wheelchair thus providing ready access to flies and tools. The cast carriers described in chapter 3 will facilitate changing flies and leaders. There's no question that answering the angling needs of a disabled child is an excellent way to exercise your ingenuity!

THE ULTIMATE CHALLENGE

For many disabled children, the foremost obstacle to fly-fishing is not physical or geographic but psychological. I refer here to the fear of failure. Overcoming this fear may pose more challenge than hooking and landing the wiliest trout. Unfortunately, many chronically disabled children have an understandable basis for their fear. They have been confronted with the discrepancy between what they and their healthy peers can do for so long that when something as novel as fly-fishing presents itself, they are apt to think, "Well, here's something else that I won't be able to do." What's called for at this moment is not an unrealistic expectation for a miracle medicine or operation—we would gladly prefer those over all other options if they were available—but rather a patient and understanding advocate who can guide them to the lasting pleasures of the pond and stream.

Donating some of your time to teach disabled children has got to be one of the most fulfilling activities ever devised. It beats by miles our comparatively dubious pastimes, such as cruising the malls, being sedated by television, trying to sleep when we're not tired or to eat when we're not hungry. It's no secret that teaching is a two-way street, and the children you meet and the experiences you share will become a permanent part of your inner resource. It can be as simple as calling the Child Life Service of your nearest children's hospital, and telling them that you'd like to share your fishing or fly-tying ability. And then, let the wonder begin.

co

CHAPTER TEN

STEWARDSHIP

"Fly fishing takes place in settings of unparalleled but often fragile beauty, and fly fishers have been in the forefront of efforts to protect naturally-flowing rivers and streams, and their fish and insect populations."

from the exhibition *Anglers All: Humanity in Midstream,*
Peabody Museum of Natural History, Yale University,
in conjunction with The American Museum of Fly Fishing,
December 15, 1992–April 18, 1993.

Childhood is not too early to assume stewardship of a stream or pond. At first this may sound a bit extreme, but we are not expecting the child to shoulder the legendary responsibilities of a Frank Sawyer on the River Avon. Stewardship is a complex role that can be fulfilled in different ways by many people, each to his own capacity. And if the child has taken up the fly rod, he has a priori shaken hands with nature, thus sealing an agreement to both understand and protect her many wonders. For fly-fishing can be conceived in no other way; this concept has been at the root of its heritage and also guides its future.

In this chapter we will explore how the child, under your guidance, can meet the terms of this almost sacred covenant. But doing so is not a grim business; it can be a source of excitement and satisfaction for the entire family. For your child to be in a position to help his chosen stream or pond, he must be equipped with some fundamental knowledge of the watershed's physical, chemical, and biological characteristics. No matter how complex they are, with your help they can be construed in terms that he can readily understand. He must then recognize how alterations of these characteristics signal threats to the stream's welfare, much the same way certain types of chest pain can warn of an impending heart attack. Finally, he must know how to administer the correct remedies or, failing that, how to summon the proper help to address the stream's ailments. From these efforts should emerge a style of comportment when he is on the water, a style that, consciously or not, he will largely pattern after you, his teacher.

Having some basic equipment on hand will facilitate your child's stewardship activities (table 10.1). These items are all inexpensive, and are described below. Let's first address your child's appreciation of the stream environment, and then discuss his conduct on the water.

THE STREAM ENVIRONMENT

Some of the Road Quizzes given in appendix A will give your child a basic idea of the physical characteristics of a stream, the workings of the water cycle, and how man's efforts can screw the cycle up. To put these in a dynamic perspective, bring her to the water to measure stream depth and flow.

Stream depth can be measured very easily using a sounding lead and a calibrated line. For the lead, get a two-pound sinker used for saltwater fishing. Attach a 10- or 20- foot length of the type of braided nylon line available in most hardware stores. The exact length of the line will be determined by the type of water you plan to sound. Use an indelible marker to mark the line every foot. The line can be wound onto one of those cheap plastic frames used to store electric extension cords. She can use this device to learn how riffles, runs, and pools differ in depth. By taking serial measurements at the same location over time, she will become attuned to how stream depth alters with the seasons and how it is affected by sudden changes such as rainstorms.

Although precise determination of stream flow can be made using elaborate streamside measurements and complex mathematical formulae, the kids can have a grand time just by tossing a bobber, leaf, or stick into the stream and, using the second hand of a watch, timing how long it

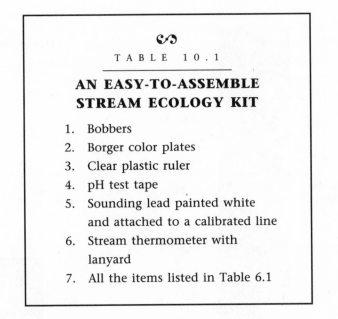

TABLE 10.1

AN EASY-TO-ASSEMBLE STREAM ECOLOGY KIT

1. Bobbers
2. Borger color plates
3. Clear plastic ruler
4. pH test tape
5. Sounding lead painted white and attached to a calibrated line
6. Stream thermometer with lanyard
7. All the items listed in Table 6.1

takes to get to a predetermined finish line. Such "races" will stimulate their competitive spirit and can become quite lively. It's best if you are the one keeping time not only to avoid arguments, but also so you can be stationed at the finish line to recover the floating items. Comparing races conducted in riffles, runs, and pools will introduce your children to how streambed contours govern flow.

Measurements of stream depth and flow can open the door to all sorts of interesting discussions, such as how deep pools are necessary to provide holdover areas for fish in times of drought, and how the filling of wetlands promotes stream flooding. I am impressed at how "grown-up" my children feel when we go out to take these measurements, and our activities inevitably spark the curiosity of other anglers and nature lovers who fall easily into conversation with us.

The waters that your children are sounding can be investigated further by both chemical and biological means. Let's look at each of these in turn.

CHEMICAL MONITORING

The simplest chemical determinations are pH, sedimentation, turbidity, and, as an indirect measure of dissolved oxygen, temperature.

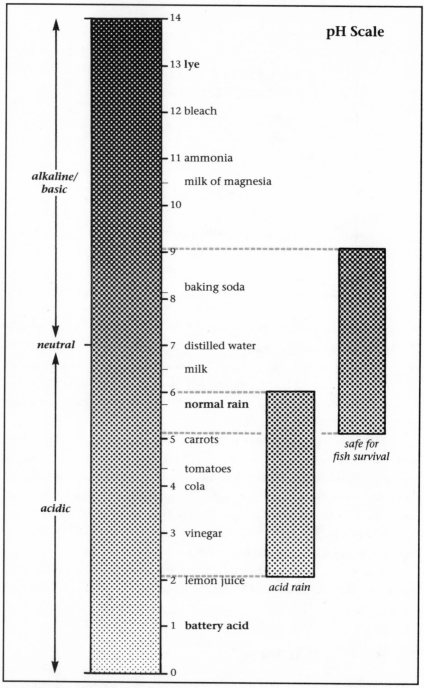

Fig. 10.1. The pH scale.

pH

pH stands for "parts hydrogen" and refers to the acidity or alkalinity of a solution (fig. 10.1). A pH of 7.0 is neutral, neither acidic nor alkaline. pH values falling below 7.0 indicate increasing acidity, while values rising above 7.0 reflect increasing alkalinity. If a solution that is very acidic (low pH) or very alkaline (high pH) were to touch your skin, you would sustain a chemical burn. The pH of your blood is carefully regulated around 7.4. If your blood pH were allowed to travel too high or too low, imagine what would happen to your insides.

Fish also have relatively narrow pH requirements. Streams supporting healthy fish populations have water pH values between 6.0 and 8.5. Trout like water on the slightly alkaline side, which is why the chalk streams of England and the limestone creeks of this country are such great places to go fishing. pH values below 4.0–4.5 wipe out most fish and aquatic insects.

Your kids can measure stream pH inexpensively by using those test strips sold by most biological supply houses. They are a lot less messy and are easier to store than methods that employ various titration reagents, and they are a tiny fraction of the cost of battery-operated pH meters.

Although swamp drainage can produce a naturally low pH, values less than 6.0 usually spell trouble. Causes include acid rain, drainage from mines, and algae overgrowth. To sort these possibilities out, check the pH of rainwater collected in a clean jar after a heavy storm, inquire whether the watershed encompasses any abandoned mines, and compare the stream pH in the morning and evening. If the difference in values is more than 0.5 units (you will need narrow range pH paper for this particular determination) then the algae are running amok. This is because algae release carbon dioxide at night and eat it up during the day. Since carbon dioxide forms an acid when it combines with water, the stream's lowest pH is usually in the early morning, while the highest pH occurs around sunset.

SEDIMENTS

During a walk along the stream with your child, ask him to identify the principal types of streambed sediments at each of several locations. Table 10.2 can be used as a guide. Panning the stream bottom with a white plastic dish, similar to the way prospectors pan for gold, is a helpful way to sort out the smaller-sized particles, and a clear plastic ruler can be used

❧

TABLE 10.2

STREAMBED SEDIMENTS

SEDIMENT TYPE	SIZE
Boulder	More than 10 inches
Cobble	2½–10 inches
Gravel	¼–2½ inches
Sand	1/16–¼ inch
Silt	Less than 1/16 inch

(Information in this table and in figures 10.2 and 10.3 is based on material kindly provided by Richard D. Klein and the Maryland Department of Natural Resources' Save Our Streams Program.)

if necessary to take the measurements. He may wish to make a map of the stream in his field journal, sketching in the regional changes in streambed composition and adding the depth and current flow measurements he determined earlier.

Use this activity to help explain how excessive siltation fills the interstices among the larger sediment types, thus smothering fish eggs and depriving aquatic insects of their breeding grounds. Ask him about the consequences to the fishery if the trout are deprived of their major food source and if there are insufficient newborn trout to replace the older ones who are dying off.

TURBIDITY

Sediment not only rests on the streambed, it also is suspended in the water, where it is measured as turbidity. You can buy turbidimeters that cost hundreds, even thousands of dollars, but it is not necessary to go that far. Simply take your sounding lead (described above) and paint it white. Now have your child lower the lead into the stream and note on the calibrated line the depth at which the lead disappears from view. The greater the depth, the less turbid is the water. Tell your kids that excess turbidity is bad news. Suspended particles can screen out sunlight needed by plants growing on the streambed, abrade the tender gills of fishes, and absorb heat from the sun, thus causing the water temperature to rise to dangerous levels (see below). Furthermore, suspended particles can act like minuscule taxicabs, transporting pesticides and other toxic substances throughout the stream. If your stream seems excessively turbid, look for adjoining areas of soil erosion or heavy fertilizer use. The latter results in excessive nutrients leaching or running off into the stream. This will promote an overgrowth of bacteria and algae that also adds to the turbidity.

DISSOLVED OXYGEN

There are many different kits available to measure the water's dissolved oxygen, and many of them contain reagents that require careful handling. Your child can get a rough estimate of dissolved oxygen, however, by simply taking the stream's temperature. This is because cold water holds more oxygen than warm water. Dissolved oxygen is important for many reasons, not the least of which is that fish need it for survival. Their requirements are quite narrow. In general, natural trout waters do not go above 68°F (20°C), recreational trout waters do not exceed 75°F (24°C), and warmwater species require water below 90°F (32°C). If the temperature exceeds these limits, the fish have two choices: They either migrate to cooler waters or, if this is not possible, they die.

Taking the time to monitor stream temperature will not only tell you if the stream has a thermal problem, it will also tell you where to fish. The optimum temperature range for brook trout is 48°F–70°F (9°C–21°C), and for rainbow and brown trout is 50°F–73°F (10°C–23°C). Fishing for these species where the water temperature exceeds these limits is pretty much a waste of time.

High-quality stream thermometers can be purchased at tackle stores for little cost. Ours is housed in a metal sleeve to prevent breakage. You will also need a lanyard. Ours is a boot lace that is tied to a ring at the top of the thermometer using a Duncan loop.

Be sure your child knows the right way to take water temperature. Choose a shaded spot so that the sun is not shining directly on the thermometer. If you are concerned that the stream may have a thermal problem, take the reading between four and five o'clock in the afternoon, since that's when the water is warmest. If you are in a stream rather than a lake or pond, place the thermometer in a riffle section so that there is good water circulation around the bulb. Hold the lanyard and lower the thermometer into the water to a point that is just above the bottom. Make sure the thermometer is not so close to your body that it will pick up your own radiant heat. Keep it there for three minutes, or the time it takes to recite the 51st Psalm. Only then remove it from the water to take your reading.

If, in your thermal investigations, you discover that your stream has a problem, enlist your children to help you discover where it's coming from. Any heated water releases from below dams should be reported to your Water Resources Administration. This recommendation may surprise you if you've read about those wonderful tail-water fisheries. In those cases however, water releases are almost always from below the dam. Dams increase the water's surface area exposed to the sun's rays, and when releases are from the top of the lake, thermal stress on the stream can be significant. High temperatures can also be due to lack of streamside vegetation. This reaches its worst when streambanks are lined with boulders and other riprap. During the summer months when the water level recedes, the boulders heat up in the sun. If there is a flash rainstorm, the water level rapidly rises and covers the heated boulders. This is akin to throwing tons of heated charcoal into the river. Water temperatures skyrocket, killing fish and aquatic insects. If your streambeds can use some plantings, contact your local Agricultural Extension Service to determine what type of vegetation would be best. Some Extension Services will supply seedlings free of charge.

COLOR AND ODOR

While we're on the subject of water quality, let's not forget the simplest of determinations, color and odor. Color is best appreciated by lowering your white plastic dish into the water and just gazing at it. If you want to get really exact about it, you can compare the color you see with the same Gary Borger Color System plates that are used for matching aquatic insects. There is a lot of overlap among causes of certain colors. For example, a yellowish brown color can be produced by soil erosion, certain algae, and dissolved organic substances. On the other hand, different algae can produce colors as varied as red, blue, and green. Hence, color determinations become most useful when used in conjunction with biological and other chemical assays.

For odor determination one uses, as the French say, le nez. Not all of us are equipped with a discriminating nez, so this is one of the more subjective measurements used in stream monitoring. Unfortunately, industry has wreaked such havoc on our streams that one can have a totally indiscriminate nez and still come away from the water positively offended. If the stream smells like a swimming pool, there is probable chlorine contamination. A fishy odor could mean dead fish, but more commonly it means lots of dead algae. If the stream smells like the part of your garage floor right underneath your car's oil pan, suspect pollution by hydrocarbons. If it smells like the rest room in a New York City subway, think raw sewage, including human and animal waste. I need not belabor this point; just writing this makes me faintly ill.

OTHER VARIABLES
A wide variety of testing kits are available for assaying other water quality factors such as hardness, nutrients, nitrate, phosphate, and salinity. If you are of a scientific bent and the kids are too, these kits, particularly the ones specifically designed for use by primary and secondary school students, may make very worthwhile investments. The kits are not toys, so adult supervision and proper safety precautions are necessary. Two sources are the Hach Company, P.O. Box 389, Loveland, Colorado 80539 or 1313 Border Street, Unit 34, Winnipeg, Manitoba, Canada R3H 0X4, and the LaMotte Company, P.O. Box 329, Chestertown, Maryland 21620. (LaMotte products are sold in Canada by Northwest Laboratories, Ltd. at P.O. Box 1356, Guelph, Ontario N1H 6N8 or P.O. Box 6100 Station C, Victoria, British Columbia V8P 5L4.) If you're looking for a tidy and readable overview of this area, order a copy of *The Monitor's Handbook* from LaMotte.

BIOLOGICAL MONITORING

In chapter 6 we discussed how to go about collecting insects and other critters from the stream. Being able to identify them offers one level of satisfaction, but understanding their ecological significance opens the door to a new world of knowledge and adventure. In general, healthier waters promote a greater diversity of insect life. Using fig. 10.2 as a guide, your children can examine their yield when kick seining and gain a rough idea of how their stream is doing. For another clue, they should identify the pollution tolerance of the recovered organisms (table 10.3). Using the *Insect and Crustacean Identification Card* offered by the Izaak Walton League of America (IWLA) greatly facilitates this process.

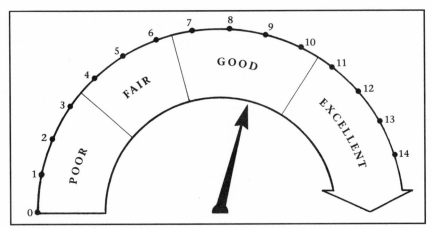

Fig. 10.2. The number of different kinds of aquatic insects found in your seine offers a general idea of water quality.

Biological monitoring need not end with insects and crustaceans. Let's not forget those tiny one-celled or multicelled plants called algae or, as my kids collectively refer to them, slime. If you thought that trying to identify the genera and species of aquatic insects was difficult, try it with algae and you'll really get a migraine. For the sake of our mutual sanity, we will steer clear of the nomenclature.

Contrary to popular belief, not all algae are bad. Insects and fish do eat the stuff. But like too much turkey on Thanksgiving, an excess is not welcome, and like the Brussels sprouts that you should have avoided,

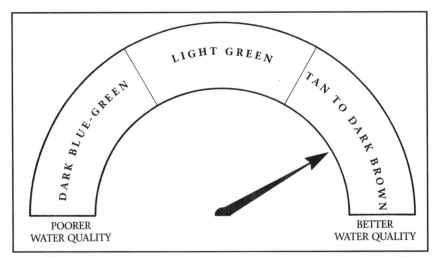

Fig. 10.3. The color of the dominant algae species also gives a clue to water quality.

TABLE 10.3

POLLUTION TOLERANCE
OF AQUATIC ORGANISMS*

REQUIRE CLEAN WATER: caddisfly, dobsonfly, gilled snail, mayfly, riffle beetle, stonefly, water penny

CAN LIVE IN GOOD- TO FAIR-QUALITY WATER: alderfly larvae, beetle larvae, clam, cranefly, crayfish, damselfly, dragonfly, fish fly larvae, scud, sowbug, watersnipe fly larvae

CAN SURVIVE IN POLLUTED OR CLEANER WATER: aquatic worm, blackfly larvae, leech, pond snail, pouch snail, midge fly larvae

*For illustrations of these organisms, consult the
Insect and Crustacean Identification Card offered by
the Izaak Walton League of America (chapter 6).*

there are certain types that are just plain bad news. Unless they form confluent nets or webs, free-swimming algae will not be captured by the kick-seine net. They are so small that their passing through the net openings is akin to our driving through the Holland Tunnel in a Buick. They will be captured by a fine-mesh plankton net, but such devices are big bucks. Scraping the stuff off of streambed rocks and transferring it to your white plastic dish is the simplest way to go about it.

You've got an algae problem if more than 10 percent of the surface area of a riffle is covered with the stuff. In addition, the color of the most predominant type of algae can give a clue to stream quality (fig. 10.3). A major cause of excess algae is organic enrichment of the stream by human sewage or lawn fertilizers. Oxygen depletion results from the decomposition of both the organic contaminants and the algae themselves. And without oxygen, you know what happens to the fish. Means of combatting the organic enrichment problem can be found in the publication *Preservation and Enhancement of Stream Quality* written by Richard D. Klein for the Maryland Department of Natural Resources' Save Our Streams

Program. While you're at it, pick up a copy of *Hands on Streams and Rivers* by the same author. Both are distributed at low cost by the IWLA.

GOING OFFICIAL

The above refers to casual stream monitoring as a family activity. You can formalize your efforts, and be more assured that your findings will lead to positive action by participating in the Save Our Streams Program sponsored by the IWLA. This program, touched on briefly in chapters 4 and 7, enables individuals, families, and organizations to preserve our nation's water quality by adopting a stream of their choice and agreeing to monitor it for a year or more. This is a great way to simultaneously have fun with the family, learn a great deal about stream ecology, and improve our environment. For little cost the IWLA will send you the Save Our Streams adoption kit that includes detailed information on how to identify harmful stream conditions and ways to combat them. Stream Quality Survey Forms to enter your data are included, and you are provided with a card to register your project with Monitors, the national S.O.S. database. Registered participants receive *Splash*, a quarterly newsletter describing successful S.O.S. projects as well as additional project ideas. The *Save Our Streams* video is also available. This describes in entertaining detail how biological monitoring is used to assess water quality. This video is appropriate for viewing in the home as well as at club and organization meetings.

WETLANDS

With our lakes, rivers, and streams in need of so much attention, asking our young anglers to turn their attention to wetlands might seem like spreading things a little too thin. Not so. Although relatively little fly-fishing goes on in wetlands, caring about and for them is very relevant to our sport. In addition to providing habitat for fish and wildlife, wetlands improve the quality of lakes and streams by filtering waste and sediment. They also help prevent soil erosion, mitigate flood damage, and replenish groundwater supplies. The IWLA is active in this area as well. Their Wetlands Watch Kit will give you and your family a firm grounding of how wetlands function and how they can be restored and enhanced. It will also guide you through the relevant legislation, most notably Section

404 of the Clean Water Act, the federal law that regulates the filling of wetlands. The kit includes the circular *Wetlands Are For Kids, Too!* that provides an excellent way to introduce this subject to your brood.

SPREADING OUT

One of the keenest ways to sharpen your child's awareness of the fragility of our environment is to make sure she understands what's out there. There's little chance that this will occur if her primary contact with the outdoors is through the window of a car racing to get to a place where she will spend time indoors.

The angling and ecology activities previously discussed are meant to enhance your delivery of this understanding. And although catching fish will be your foremost interest on most outings, welcome the children's attraction to other activities that the watershed provides. This may include bird watching, making plaster of Paris molds of animal tracks, wildflower and tree identification, hikes, kite flying, orienteering with map and compass, scavenger hunts, outdoor photography, and of course camping. One of our fondest memories was our discovery of a beautiful yellow wildflower on the banks of our beloved Willimantic during one of our fishing excursions. We consulted our field guide and were delighted to learn that its speckled petals had earned it the name Trout Lily.

SCHOOL

Wouldn't it be fortunate if your children's school was able to reinforce the concepts of stewardship that you are introducing at home? You may be able to make this happen by directing their teachers' attention to the California Trout, Salmon and Steelhead Education Program, a special curriculum devised by Diane Higgins for children in grades kindergarten through six. This curriculum has been brought to the classrooms of 25,000 students, largely through the guidance of David Armocido, an educator who is also a fisherman and the organizer of the Colusa County Chapter of Trout Unlimited. Each class is given 50 fertilized steelhead eggs that hatch in a classroom aquarium. The students learn about the life cycle of the fish as well as its habitat requirements. The students' aquarium observations are supplemented by field trips to nearby rivers, and they ultimately release into the river the steelhead that they have nurtured to young adulthood. Information about the program can be obtained from David Armocido, 232 Cynthia Drive, Colusa, California 95932.

CONDUCT ASTREAM

Child psychologists hammer home the concept that children learn more from their parents' actions than from their words. Time spent with children on the water gives parents an exceptional opportunity to capitalize on this principle and also to refine their own stream etiquette. Let's begin with one of our biggest mutual concerns.

LITTER

Let's face it, if the kids see you snip off some leader material and toss it into the stream, they will do likewise, and so will their own children someday. You've instantly created an unbroken legacy of trash. To see how all of this adds up, consult table 10.4. Some companies sell little receptacles for monofilament waste that can be attached to your clothing. These are hardly necessary. You can just as easily dedicate a pocket of your vest, shirt, or jeans for this purpose. I happen to prefer the chest pocket on my waders. Before we head for the water, instead of lecturing my kids not to litter, I ask them to show me what pocket they've selected on their own clothing for waste disposal that day.

Another trick I learned from a park ranger on Block Island. One bright summer morning, we met her to go on a nature walk near the lovely lighthouse on the northernmost tip of the island. She was a veritable repository of fascinating knowledge, and as she held us under her spell, she unceremoniously extracted a trash bag from her backpack. Without interrupting her discourse or her stride, she swooped down and scooped up bits of litter that were scattered over the dunes and beach grass. Sure enough, the rest of us began pitching in, without a single request from her to do so. The activity did not in the slightest interfere with our appreciation of the walk. In fact, just the reverse was true. We all felt really good about leaving the place a little cleaner than when we had arrived.

Now when I go fishing with my children, a trash bag is kept folded in the back pocket of my fishing vest. At the end of the day, as we head

ℰℐ

T A B L E   1 0 . 4

HOW LONG COMMONLY DISCARDED ITEMS TAKE TO DECOMPOSE

Paper	2–4 months
Orange peels	6 months
Wool socks	1–5 years
Milk cartons, coffee cups	5 years
Filter cigarettes	10–12 years
Plastic bags	10–20 years
Disposable diapers	10–20 years
Leather shoes	25–40 years
Nylon fabric	30–40 years
Sneaker sole	50–80 years
Tin cans	80–100 years
Aluminum cans and tabs	200–400 years
Plastic six-pack holder	450 years
Glass bottles	1 million years
Styrofoam	indefinitely
Plastic bottles	indefinitely
Monofilament line	indefinitely

(Data kindly provided by David Diligent, Cornell Cooperative Extension.)

back to the car, I extract the bag and emulate the park ranger. And my children do pitch in, with nary a word from me.

Another positive step you can take is to read to your children Munro Leaf's book *Who Cares? I Do* (Scholastic Book Services, New York, 1972). This eloquent diatribe against littering and defacement of public and private property is replete with startling photos documenting man's indifference to his environment. The photos were supplied by the U.S. Forest Service, the National Park Service, and Keep America Beautiful, Inc.

TURN IN POACHERS
1 - 800 - 842 - HELP
24 HOURS TOLL FREE

TIP of Connecticut Inc. • P.O. Box 503
Marlborough, Connecticut 06447

STATE OF CONNECTICUT

HELP US HELP YOU RECORD THE FOLLOWING:
Violation _____
Time _____ Date _____
Vehicle_____ Lic. # _____
State _____ Color _____
Violator: Sex _____ Age _____
Ht. _____ Wt. _____
Hair _____ Eyes _____
Identifying marks or features: _____

Fig. 10.4. Bandits beware.

POACHERS

There are some sour truths that children must learn on the path to adulthood. These include all the awful "p" words: pain, pestilence, plague, and poachers. No doubt the unlawful taking of fish, particularly in fly-fishing-only zones, has made you bristle on more than one occasion. Having your children witness your counterattack can leave them with some very vivid impressions.

Here in Connecticut we have a Turn In Poachers Program that provides a nonconfrontational way of dealing with this problem (Figure 10-4). It works like this. You and your kids are astream. You see someone spin-casting some meat in a fly-fishing-only area. You inform your children that this is unlawful activity, go to the nearest phone (a problem if you are in the backwoods of Montana, but not if you're in Connecticut), call a designated number, inform the TIP representative of the mischief, and a conservation officer is dispatched to the river to expel and fine the offender. Having your kids observe this scenario will probably be more memorable for them than the day's fishing.

A difficulty you may encounter in executing this task is remembering the phone number. George Degen of the Connecticut Fly Fishermen's Association sets a good example. He's inscribed the TIP phone number on the underside of the visor of his fishing cap for ready reference.

In the absence of a TIP system, the direct approach of confronting the unsavory offenders may be necessary. Hurling epithets and threatening physical violence is unlikely to be effective unless you look like Arnold Schwarzenegger. A more subtle tactic is described by Leonard Wright in his book *Neversink* (Atlantic Monthly Press, New York, 1991). Mr. Wright is privileged to own some very sweet water on that fabled Catskill stream. I have never met him, but I presume that he does not look like Arnold. From time to time he's had to eject poachers from his property, and his means of doing so is almost British in its spirit of high manners. On coming upon the poachers, he first cordially asks them if they've had any luck fishing. Next he asks them if they come there often. Only then, after he has charmed the whiskers off them, does he let the bombshell fall. He informs them that the area is posted and, as they recoil in embarrassment, tells them to leave. He claims great success with this method, and it has been equally successful in my hands on the fly-fishing-only stretch of the Willimantic.

There is another devastating method to deal with poachers that I hesitate to put into print lest the opposition get hold of it and render it useless. It has never failed me yet. After much self-deliberation I've decided to let you in on it. You are sworn to secrecy. Here goes. My children own toy walkie-talkies. Although inexpensive, they work very well over short distances and look like very expensive instruments. They are equipped with buttons that, when pressed, emit all manner of official sounding beeps. On spotting a poacher and reassuring myself that I am in his visual and hearing range, I whip out the walkie-talkie, produce many beeps, and then "report" the offense. The only problem with this technique is that the poachers leave the pool so fast, they put down the fish for a good 15 to 20 minutes.

RECRUITMENT

Part of the success of instilling environmental awareness in your children is having them see you enlist others for the cause. Some fly-fishers pursue this with almost religious zeal. Again I am reminded of George Degen who, when sharing a pool on the Willimantic with another angler, asks him if he's a member of the Connecticut Fly Fishermen's Association. If the answer is no, George reaches into an inside pocket of his vest and hands him a pamphlet containing a description of the club's recreational and environmental activities and an application blank for membership. Such encounters have won our organization some very valued and active members.

CATCH-AND-RELEASE

If you do not already practice catch-and-release (fig. 10.5), I'm not sure I have the eloquence to change your mind. Regardless of your personal preferences, I do believe that you owe it to your children and succeeding generations to have them practice this philosophy. I don't mean to be pushy, but I simply cannot speak calmly about this subject. I personally view the killing of any fish that is not destined to be eaten as unnecessary. If fish are removed from a body of water because overpopulation has led to the stunting of their growth, then they too should be eaten. The wanton killing of fish is, like smoking, an open manifestation of man's ignorance and propensity for self-destruction. Although such killing does not destroy man's own flesh, it does rob him of a valuable indicator species that tells him how he's doing and where he's headed. And panfish are no exception. My reaction to such killing is visceral, the way I feel when driving on the turnpike through Elizabeth, New Jersey and I attempt to breathe.

There's been recent talk of taking catch-and-release one step further: "tag" fishing with the Touch And Go hooks available from the venerable firm of Partridge in Redditch, England. These hooks have two eyes: one where you'd expect it to be, and the other in place of the point and barb. The angler can thus feel the strike without the hook penetrating the fish. Although he cannot expect to land such "tagged" fish, he can experience the momentary connection with wildness that constitutes the central core of fly-fishing. It's too early to tell where this movement will go, but I'm watching with extreme interest, and intend to try some tag fishing with my children this coming season.

A sublime way of introducing the concept of catch-and-release to your children is to read them Allen Say's evocative book *A River Dream* (Houghton Mifflin Company, Boston, 1988). The book is a beautiful marriage of text and artwork, and the images thus conjured will stay with you and your children long after the book is put down.

THE BIG PICTURE

Although we have discussed stewardship as a separate entity in this chapter, it merges imperceptibly with all of the other topics that we discussed earlier. This is part of the seamless beauty of fly-fishing, a beauty that renews itself each time we venture to the stream to meet new challenges. And in the end fly-fishing, like life, consists of a series of decisions. Is it safe to wade over to that distant rock? Should I tie on an Adams? Should I kill or release the fish? Some of the decisions will be so

Fig. 10.5. One's youth is an outstanding time in life to become acquainted with the principles of catch-and-release.

easy that we will act on them instinctively, before they are even fully articulated in our consciousness. Others will be more difficult. And for these it is helpful to have a code or set of guidelines, regardless of whether you are the student or the instructor. Here is one family's code.

A CHILD'S TEN RULES OF FLY-FISHING

1. I will always wear my cap and glasses when I am casting and when I am near anyone who is casting.
2. I will only wade with adult supervision, and I will obey the rules of safe wading (chapter 5).
3. I will use only barbless hooks.
4. For all fish not meant to be eaten, I will practice catch-and-release.
5. I will not litter.
6. I will not be profane, and I will respect the rights of other anglers.
7. I will be familiar with my local fishing regulations.
8. I will not engage in risky behavior whether on or near the water.
9. I will work hard in my life to preserve and restore our natural resources.
10. I will not be a fly-fishing snob. This is our earth, and we're all in this together.

TEN RULES FOR THE TEACHING PARENTS

1. Rig all tackle the night before.
2. Begin with bluegill.
3. Fish as you would have your children fish.
4. Know the specific water you are fishing before bringing your kids to it.
5. When you are teaching your kids how to fish, don't fish yourself.
6. Provide safe, alternative activities for the child who needs a break from fishing. This need is not a crime.
7. Carry a first-aid kit and know how to use it.
8. Patience is the golden virtue. Corollary: Don't be disappointed if your kid does not cast like Lefty; neither do you.
9. Enroll your child in an organization with high conservation standards, such as Trout Unlimited and the Federation of Fly Fishers.
10. Share your knowledge with disabled children, and encourage your children to do the same.

જી

Good fishing. And as your lines tighten, so may your relationship with your children.

അ

ROAD QUIZZES

TACKLE TIME!

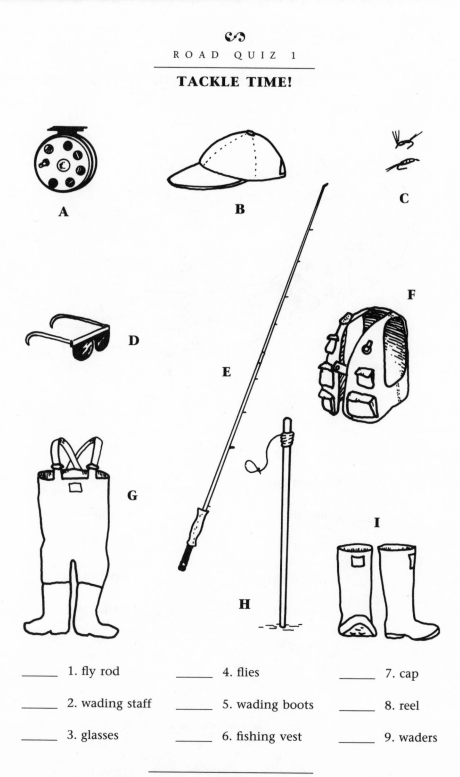

_____ 1. fly rod   _____ 4. flies   _____ 7. cap

_____ 2. wading staff   _____ 5. wading boots   _____ 8. reel

_____ 3. glasses   _____ 6. fishing vest   _____ 9. waders

MR. AND MRS. FISH

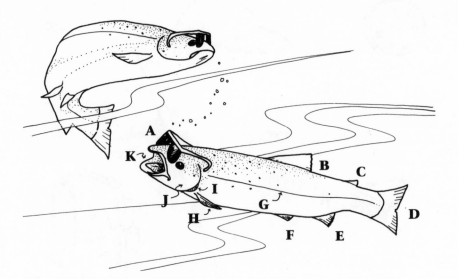

_____ 1. lateral line

_____ 2. mouth

_____ 3. dorsal fin

_____ 4. caudal (tail) fin

_____ 5. pectoral fin

_____ 6. gill cover

_____ 7. gill

_____ 8. adipose fin

_____ 9. shades

_____ 10. pelvic fin

_____ 11. anal fin

✿

STREAMSIDE KNOW-HOW!

1. The two articles of clothing I should
   always wear when I am casting or when
   I am near someone who is casting are _____

   and _____ .

2. When I go fishing, it's OK to litter.   True _____   False _____

3. I should try to release all my fish
   unharmed unless I am going to
   have them for dinner.   True _____   False _____

4. When I am casting, I should look all
   around me to be sure there is no one
   near me whom I might snag.   True _____   False _____

5. If I come to a stream or pond and I see
   other people fishing, I should whoop
   and holler and jump up and down.   True _____   False _____

6. It's best to use barbless hooks or
   have an adult remove the barbs
   from my hooks.   True _____   False _____

7. I should work hard to keep our
   air clean, our water pure, and our
   planet safe.   True _____   False _____

8. When assembling my tackle, it's
   OK to lay the reel on the ground.   True _____   False _____

9. When I am finished fishing, I should
   wipe down my rod with a dry towel
   before putting it away.   True _____   False _____

10. After fishing, what do I do with my reel? _____

    _____

11. Fishing is awesome.   True _____   False _____

ᑫᓌ

ROAD QUIZ 4

IT'S CAPTAIN HOOK!

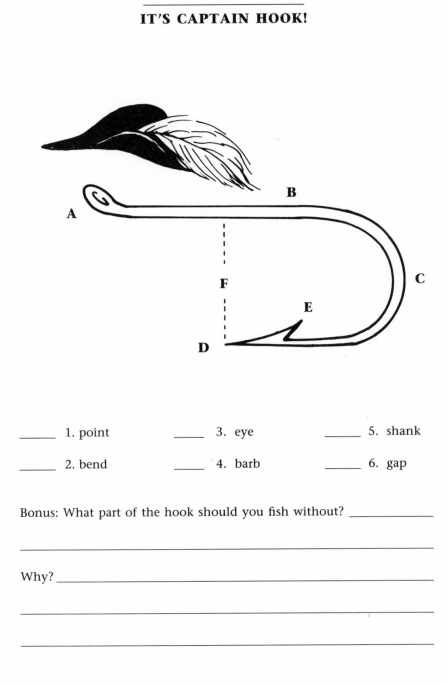

_____ 1. point	_____ 3. eye	_____ 5. shank
_____ 2. bend	_____ 4. barb	_____ 6. gap

Bonus: What part of the hook should you fish without? _____

_____

Why? _____

_____

_____

ROAD QUIZ 5

NAME THE PARTS OF THIS FLY ROD!

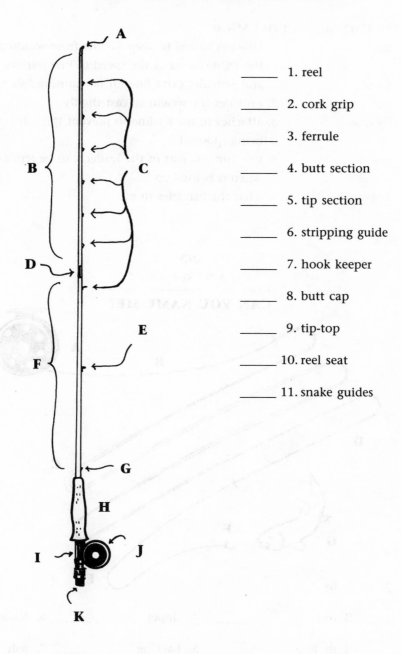

_____ 1. reel

_____ 2. cork grip

_____ 3. ferrule

_____ 4. butt section

_____ 5. tip section

_____ 6. stripping guide

_____ 7. hook keeper

_____ 8. butt cap

_____ 9. tip-top

_____ 10. reel seat

_____ 11. snake guides

ɛↄ

ROAD QUIZ 6

MATCH COLUMN A WITH COLUMN B!

COLUMN A	COLUMN B
fly	1. attaches to reel to keep fly line from winding too tight, increases the speed of line retrieve, and provides extra line for far-running fish
backing	
	2. provides the weight to cast the fly
fly line	3. attaches to the fly line to prevent the fish from being spooked
leader	4. the thinnest part of the leader; can be replaced when it is used up
tippet	5. what the fish tries to eat

ɛↄ

ROAD QUIZ 7

CAN YOU NAME ME?

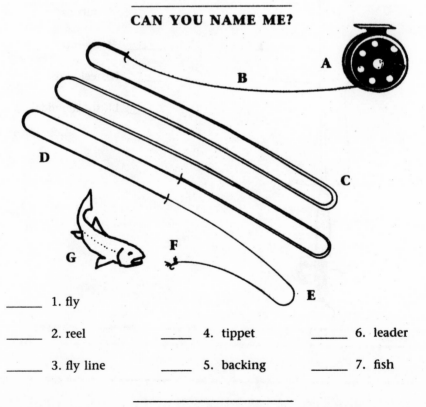

_____ 1. fly

_____ 2. reel   _____ 4. tippet   _____ 6. leader

_____ 3. fly line   _____ 5. backing   _____ 7. fish

ᏋᏕ

WHO ARE THESE BUGS?

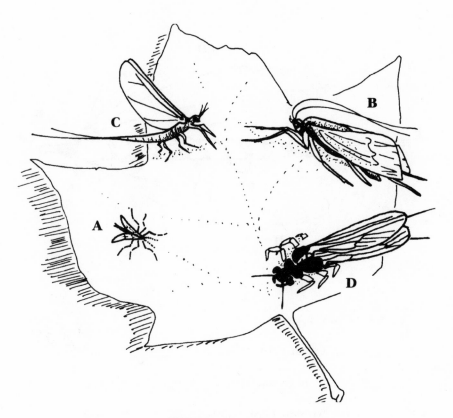

HINTS:

_____	1. mayfly	Wings stand up like sails on sailboats.
_____	2. stone fly	Wings lie flat on back.
_____	3. caddis fly	Wings are tent-shaped, like a moth's.
_____	4. midge	Fly is small like a mosquito, but doesn't bite.

ROAD QUIZ 9

THE ARTIFICIAL FLY

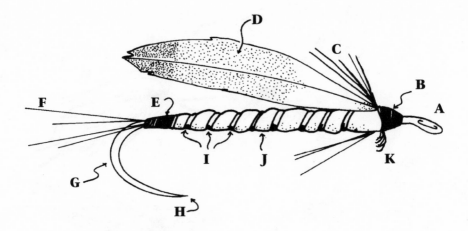

NAME MY PARTS!

_____	1. eye of hook	_____	7. beard
_____	2. bend of hook	_____	8. wing
_____	3. barbless hook point	_____	9. hackle
_____	4. head	_____	10. ribbing
_____	5. body	_____	11. tag
_____	6. tail		

(Note: Not every fly will have ALL of these parts!)

ℰꙮ

MATCH COLUMN A WITH COLUMN B!

COLUMN A

wet fly

nymph

dry fly

streamer

COLUMN B

1. a fly that floats on top of the water
2. a fly that imitates baitfish (small fish that larger fish eat)
3. a fly that imitates an immature insect (a young insect that hasn't developed its wings yet)
4. a fly that swims under the surface of the water, usually representing an emerging or a drowned insect

ℰꙮ

NAME THAT FLY!

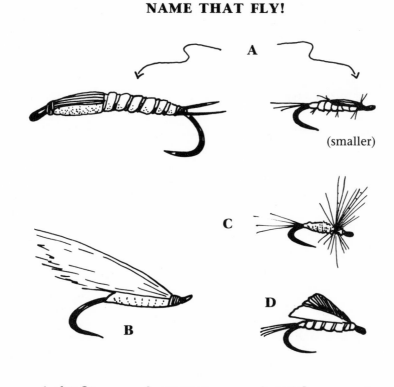

A

(smaller)

C

B

D

_____ 1. dry fly _____ 2. streamer _____ 3. wet fly _____ 4. nymph

ROAD QUIZ 12

THE FLY-TIER'S BENCH

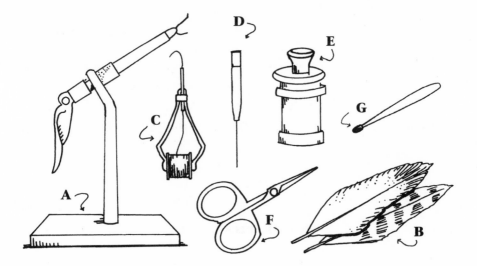

CAN YOU SORT THROUGH ALL THIS GEAR?

_____ 1. feathers		_____ 5. bobbin threader
_____ 2. scissors		_____ 6. hair stacker
_____ 3. bobbin		_____ 7. bodkin
_____ 4. vise		

WELCOME TO THE WATERSHED!

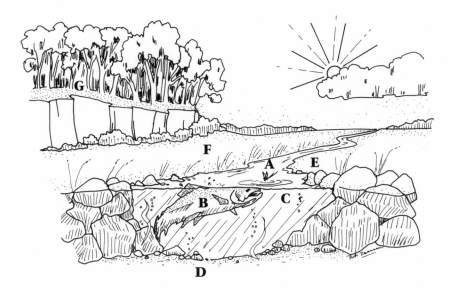

_____ 1. water

_____ 2. streambed

_____ 3. uplands

_____ 4. floodplain

_____ 5. stream bank

_____ 6. fish

_____ 7. mayfly

໙

COME ON BOARD THE WATER CYCLE!

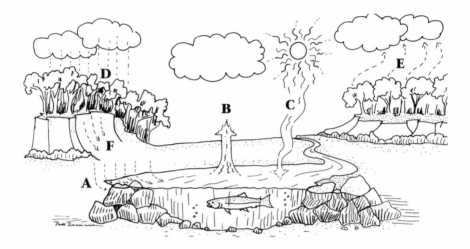

_____ 1. Rain falls from clouds.

_____ 2. Rain rushes down slopes into stream.

_____ 3. Rain sinks into ground and seeps into stream.

_____ 4. Sun's rays heat up the stream.

_____ 5. Heated water evaporates back into the air.

_____ 6. Water is also returned to air by trees through transpiration.

ℰℐ

ROAD QUIZ 15

THE ACID RAIN STORY

_____ 1. Fresh rain falls from the clouds.

_____ 2. Factories and power plants spew sulfur dioxide into the air.

_____ 3. Motor vehicles spew nitrogen oxide into the air.

_____ 4. The sulfur dioxide and the nitrogen oxide combine with the fresh rainwater to produce acid rain.

_____ 5. The acid rain falls into streams, ponds, and lakes, killing fish and other living things.

Bonus question 1: How can you test for acid rain?_____

_____

Bonus question 2: How can you prevent acid rain? _____

_____

☙

THE ANSWERS!

ROAD QUIZ 1:

    1. E; 2. H; 3. D; 4. C; 5. I; 6. F; 7. B; 8. A; 9. G

ROAD QUIZ 2:

    1. G; 2. K; 3. B; 4. D; 5. H; 6. J; 7. I; 8. C; 9. A; 10. F; 11. E

ROAD QUIZ 3:

    1. visored cap and glasses; 2. false; 3. true; 4. true; 5. false; 6. true; 7. true; 8. false; 9. true; 10. Let it air dry completely before putting it away; 11. true

ROAD QUIZ 4:

    1. D; 2. C; 3. A; 4. E; 5. B; 6. F

Bonus: the barb, because you can damage the fish if you try to remove a barbed hook, and if *you* get stuck, it's easier to remove a barbless hook, and less painful

ROAD QUIZ 5:

    1. J; 2. H; 3. D; 4. F; 5. B; 6. E; 7. G; 8. K; 9. A; 10. I; 11. C

ROAD QUIZ 6:

    1. backing; 2. fly line; 3. leader; 4. tippet; 5. fly

ROAD QUIZ 7:

    1. F; 2. A; 3. C; 4. E; 5. B; 6. D; 7. G

ROAD QUIZ 8:

    1. C; 2. D; 3. B; 4. A

ROAD QUIZ 9:

    1. A; 2. G; 3. H; 4. B; 5. J; 6. F; 7. K; 8. D; 9. C; 10. I; 11. E

ROAD QUIZ 10:

    1. dry fly; 2. streamer; 3. nymph; 4. wet fly

ROAD QUIZ 11:

    1. C; 2. B; 3. D; 4. A

ROAD QUIZ 12:

    1. B; 2. F; 3. C; 4. A; 5. G; 6. E; 7. D

ROAD QUIZ 13:

    1. C; 2. D; 3. G; 4. F; 5. E; 6. B; 7. A

ROAD QUIZ 14:

    1. D; 2. F; 3. A; 4. C; 5. B; 6. E

ROAD QUIZ 15:

    1. C; 2. E; 3. A; 4. B; 5. D

Bonus question 1: by dipping pH (litmus) paper into the water and comparing the color of the wet paper to the color chart. There are also titration methods and electronic meters to measure pH.

Bonus question 2: Car pool, use mass transit, walk or bike instead of taking the car, don't waste electricity at home, insulate your home to minimize heating and air conditioning.

PATTERNS FOR PANFISH

(All hook serial numbers are Mustad)

1. WHITE MILLER

HOOK: 3906, #10–#14

THREAD: white

TAIL: none

RIB: fine, flat silver tinsel

BODY: white floss

HACKLE: white hen

WING: white duck quill segments

COMMENT: fished wet

2. M^cGINTY

HOOK: 3906B, #10–#14

THREAD: black

TAIL: barred teal over red hackle fibers

BODY: alternate bands of yellow and black chenille

HACKLE: brown

WING: drake mallard secondaries

COMMENT: wing segments are blue with white tips

3. WOOLLY WORM

HOOK: 38941, #8–#12

THREAD: black

TAIL: red wool

RIB: silver tinsel (optional)

BODY: yellow chenille

HACKLE: grizzly palmered over body

COMMENT: colors limited only by your imagination

4. GOLD-RIBBED HARE'S EAR NYMPH

HOOK: 3906B, #10–#14

THREAD: brown

TAIL: mallard flank fibers

RIB: fine gold tinsel

BODY: hare's mask and ear dubbing

HACKLE: fur picked out from sides of thorax

WING CASE: gray duck quill segment tied over thorax

COMMENT: like the McGinty and Woolly Worm, we often fish
these weighted

5. RIO GRANDE KING

HOOK: 3906, #8–#12

THREAD: black

TAIL: yellow hackle fibers

BODY: black chenille

HACKLE: yellow

WING: white duck quill sections

6. MUDDLER MINNOW

HOOK: 38941, #8–#12

THREAD: brown

TAIL: mottled turkey quill sections

BODY: flat gold tinsel

WING: mottled turkey quill sections over gray squirrel-tail

HEAD: spun deer hair

COMMENT: when trimming the head, leave a collar of hair
extending over the body

7. FOAM-BODIED SPIDER

HOOK: 9672, #10–#12

THREAD: yellow

TAIL: short red hackle fibers

BODY: yellow foam

HACKLE: rubber legs

COMMENT: tie constrictions in the foam to define the head,
thorax, and abdomen

8. GIRDLE BUG

HOOK: 9672, #10–#12

THREAD: black

TAIL: rubber legs tied in a "V" configuration

BODY: black chenille

HACKLE: rubber legs

COMMENT: can be fished dry or weighted wet

9. CORK-BODIED POPPER

HOOK: 33903, #8–#12

THREAD: brown

TAIL: four grizzly hackles, flared outwards

BODY: shaped cork

HACKLE: grizzly tied behind cork

COMMENTS: rubber legs help; paint eyes on the cork; some fly
shops sell preshaped cork bodies

10. JOE'S HOPPER

HOOK: 9672, size #8

THREAD: brown

TAIL: red hackle fibers

BODY: brown hackle palmered over yellow chenille

HACKLE: mixed brown and grizzly

WING: mottled turkey quill sections

COMMENT: a loop of the chenille is formed over the tail

CASTING INSTRUCTIONS

1. THE ROLL CAST:

A. Strip out 20 feet of line beyond the tiptop. Hold the rod with your thumb on top of the grip and the rod pointing toward the surface of the water.

B. Bring the rod tip back so that the segment of line between rod tip and the water's surface forms a belly that is positioned *behind* your casting shoulder. Wait for the line to stop moving on the water before beginning the forward cast.

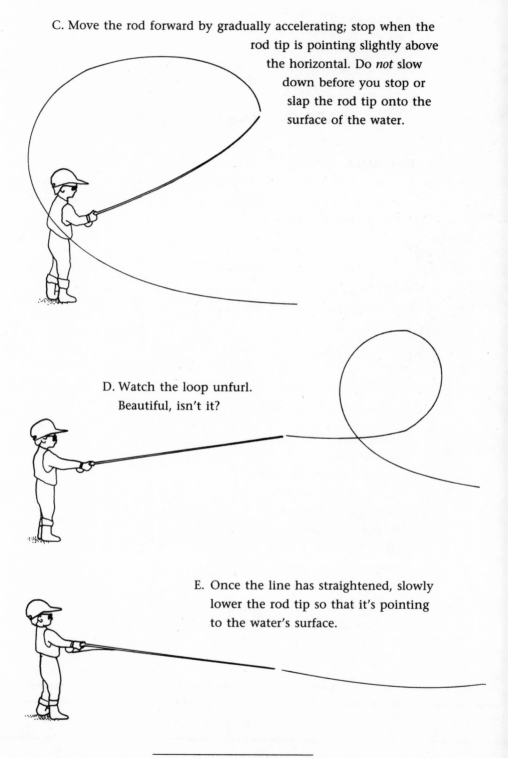

C. Move the rod forward by gradually accelerating; stop when the rod tip is pointing slightly above the horizontal. Do *not* slow down before you stop or slap the rod tip onto the surface of the water.

D. Watch the loop unfurl. Beautiful, isn't it?

E. Once the line has straightened, slowly lower the rod tip so that it's pointing to the water's surface.

2. THE BACK AND FORWARD CAST:

A. Begin as you would the roll cast, with your thumb on top of grip and the rod tip pointing down toward the water. Before bringing the rod back, be sure that there is no slack in the line. If there is, remove it by executing one or more roll casts.

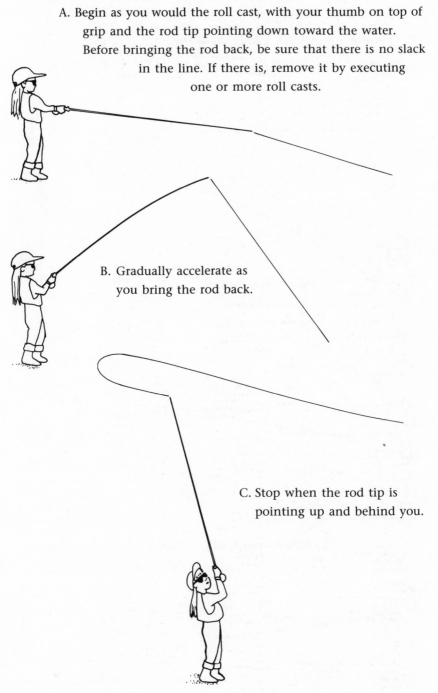

B. Gradually accelerate as you bring the rod back.

C. Stop when the rod tip is pointing up and behind you.

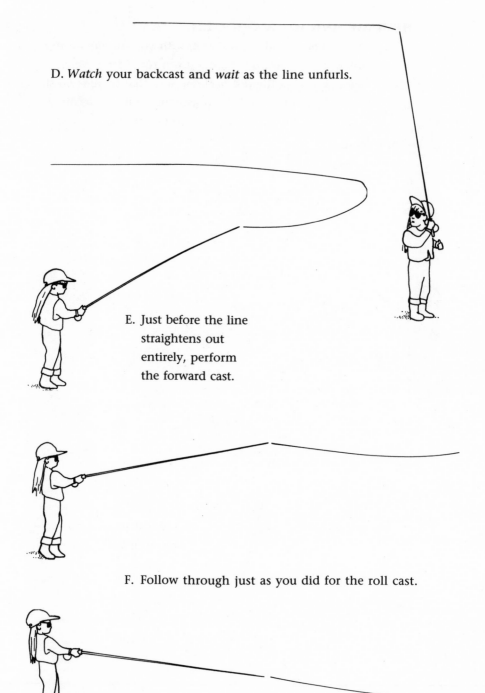

D. *Watch* your backcast and *wait* as the line unfurls.

E. Just before the line straightens out entirely, perform the forward cast.

F. Follow through just as you did for the roll cast.

3. LINE MENDING:

The example given is for an upstream mend, i.e., when the water under the line is flowing faster than the water under the fly, resulting in a belly in the line that is pointing downstream.

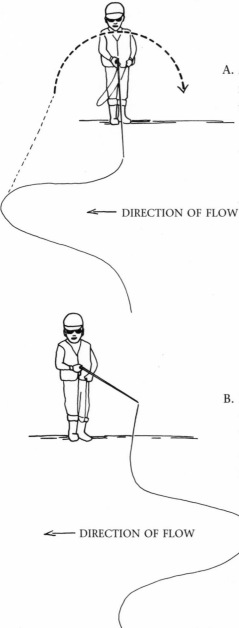

A. As with casting, start with the rod tip pointing down towards the surface of the water.

⟵ DIRECTION OF FLOW

B. Flip the rod tip in an arc towards the upstream direction. This will reverse the direction of the line belly so that it is now pointing upstream. The current must now over-come this mended position and also put another downstream belly in the line before the fly can start dragging.

⟵ DIRECTION OF FLOW

For an even longer drag-free float, you can repeatedly mend line each time the current neutralizes your mended upstream belly. This is called stack mending.

If when you mend line you wind up jerking the fly off the surface of the water, try letting out a little slack as you make the upstream arc; you'll be pleased with the results.

When the water under the line is moving slower than the water under the fly, an upstream belly forms. To avoid drag, just mend in the downstream direction. Don't fret about the actual hydraulic physics involved. Just remember to mend line in a direction *opposite* to which the line belly is forming.

INDEX

(Bold page numbers indicate illustrations)

ℰℛ

Fly-Fishing with Children

*Designed by Sally Sherman and
composed by Chelsea Dippel in Stone Serif
with illustrations by Karen Savary and Patti Zimmerman*

Printed and bound by Quebecor Printing Book Press Inc.